THE PLACE OF
FASCISM
IN EUROPEAN HISTORY

Gilbert Allardyce is Associate Professor of European History at the University of New Brunswick, Canada. A scholar and researcher on the subject of French fascism, he has also written "The Political Transition of Jacques Doriot."

THE PLACE OF
FASCISM
IN EUROPEAN HISTORY

Edited by

Gilbert Allardyce

Englewood Cliffs, N.J.   A SPECTRUM BOOK Prentice-Hall, Inc.

CONTENTS

THE PLACE OF FASCISM IN EUROPEAN HISTORY
by *Gilbert Allardyce*   1

FASCISM AS THE END OF LIBERAL SOCIETY   29

FASCISM AS THE DICTATORSHIP OF DECAYING
CAPITALISM
by *R. Palme Dutt*   29

FASCISM AS LOWER-MIDDLE-CLASS PSYCHOLOGY
by *Erich Fromm*   36

FASCISM AS THE END OF ECONOMIC MAN
by *Peter F. Drucker*   49

FASCISM AS TOTALITARIANISM   67

FASCISM AS TOTALITARIANISM: MEN AND
TECHNOLOGY
by *Carl J. Friedrich* and *Zbigniew K. Brzezinski*   67

FASCISM AS TOTALITARIANISM: IDEOLOGY AND
TERROR
by *Hannah Arendt*   86

vii

FASCISM AS A RADICAL FORM
OF TRADITIONAL POLITICAL PROTEST

95

FASCISM AS THE CONJUNCTION OF RIGHT AND LEFT
by *Eugen Weber*   95

FASCISM AS THE EXTREMISM OF THE CENTER
by *Seymour Lipset*   110

FASCISM AS THE EXTREMISM OF THE RIGHT
by *John Weiss*   121

FASCISM AS A REVOLT AGAINST
MODERNISM

127

FASCISM AS THE HERITAGE OF CONSERVATIVE
MODERNIZATION
by *Barrington Moore*   127

FASCISM AS AN ANTIMODERNIST REVOLT
by *Ernst Nolte*   144

FASCISM AS THE REVOLT OF "THE LOSERS"
by *Wolfgang Sauer*   162

SUGGESTED READINGS
ON INTERNATIONAL FASCISM

175

THE PLACE OF
FASCISM
IN EUROPEAN HISTORY

Gilbert Allardyce

THE PLACE OF FASCISM
IN EUROPEAN HISTORY

"Fascism," a historian has written, "was the great political surprise of the first half of the twentieth century." Although the nineteenth century had been full of ideological speculation, no one had foreseen the coming of fascism. And despite all the literature that has since been written to explain the movement, few scholars are convinced that they fully understand it. Fascism remains the most difficult and perhaps the most important historical problem of our time. As a political expression, it carried all the markings of a crisis in European history: the brutality of an age of total war, the desperate moods of economic catastrophe, the intransigence of classes fearful of social revolution and political disaster. But how is fascism related to this crisis in the history of the continent? What is its connection with the European past and what does its defeat mean for the future? In a word, what is the place of fascism in European history? This volume is concerned with that question.

Nothing appears more foreign to our times than the fascist years—years of marching columns, flags, and torchlight, a season when grown men indulged themselves in pagan pageantry and Roman salutes. Hitler once remarked that his movement would appear to the future as though it were a fairy tale; it appears instead like a nightmare. What we must understand, however, is that this thing which now seems so frightful and grotesque looked to many men at the time as a vision of the world that was to come. In the 1930s Europe was moving visibly toward the fulfillment of Mussolini's prophecy that the twentieth century would be an era of fascism. The verdict of the First World War was being reversed: the victors began to founder while fascism gave the vanquished a new sense of strength and direction. As the initiative passed from the parliamentary nations to the fascist dictatorships, and as each nation in turn gave rise to its own fascist organizations, every opposing political force was thrown onto the defensive. At a time when the full emergence of mass society caused free men to ponder uneasily over the future of their institutions, fascists took confidence that their own conceptions were rooted in the very nature of mass man.

In the years before the Second World War, antifascism came to dominate the political life of the democracies almost in the way that fascism dominated the political life of Germany and Italy. Yet nothing seemed to work against the dictators—neither alliances, bluster, nor appeasement. Fascism had gathered the momentum of events and everything fell away before it. Its spirit was "in the air" that Europeans breathed. One of its admirers would later remark that fascism was the *mal du siècle* of the generation that came of age between the two world wars. Certainly it forever left its impression upon those who lived in its time. To have lived through this experience was to become possessed by a political consciousness that has continued into the present. This is what it means to be "over thirty."

With the coming of the war all the intricate conditions that had nurtured the continuing development of fascism were reduced to a simple equation: its immediate future would depend upon the success of Hitler's arms. And now what is left? Few movements of such magnitude have left such meager remains. In its time fascism moved great masses, built up forceful institutions, and sent out invincible legions. It left behind only a few political parties living on the margins of public life, the fossilized remains of fascist structures in Spain, and the stragglers of defeated battalions carrying on a dialogue with death in European beerhalls. Hollow men are left to explain the substance of fascism, menial men to account for its ambitions. Even the most murderous among them appear somehow out of size with their works: monstrous deeds perpetrated by little men. We must learn to accept the difficult truth that Hitler's regime was the most popular government in German history; yet we know as well that few Germans after the war would confess having given any loyalty to the Nazi movement. This was not a lie in the soul of the German nation; it was a part of the collective delusion that all the fascist movements brought upon their followings. It was as if the movements themselves, as things independent of the men that embodied them, were responsible for the things that happened. When the movements disappeared in the holocaust, everything that had given them life and spirit were carried away with them. Fascism had raged and stormed as though it would transform an entire continent, and then there was nothing left, neither loyalties, passions, nor beliefs. A force that once appeared the elemental political expression of its age became a thing alien and incomprehensible.

Now it remains for historians to provide an understanding of fascism. For reasons that will be suggested in the following paragraphs, they have found it a difficult task. No doubt part of the problem lies in the nature of the historical method itself. Objectivity and detachment are the traditional prerequisites to the historian's craft, but no student of humanity can permit himself to be objective about the dark things that happened in fascist Europe. When these matters arise, historical discourse inevitably becomes moralistic. Yet in a way moral involvement is inseparable from an understanding of fascism, for the fascist era can be interpreted in a general sense as a study in the moral collapse of Western civilization. The full dimensions of this catastrophe are only beginning to become observable. The more deeply historians explore its causes, the wider becomes the circle of guilt and responsibility. Vast deeds of violence and excess once attributed to the perversity of the German national character or the mindless nihilism of fascist jackboots must now be conceived in a broader international context. We know now that such things could not have happened in the same way without the participation of others: without the collaboration of respected statesmen in the conquered countries, without the acquiescence of the British cabinet, the indifference of the American state department, or the silence of the Vatican. These things are difficult to say, but it is necessary to say them.

The proper study of fascism is thus of international breadth and immense philosophic depth. If the fascists were intellectually shallow in themselves, they at least were profound in their ability to reveal the moral condition of the West in the first half of the twentieth century. For although fascism has a common reputation for vulgarity and barbarousness, it could work in subtle and perplexing ways as well. It had a way of confronting its opponents with political and ethical choices of the most ponderous complexity: the choice, for instance, of delivering a foreign people to war and conquest in order to preserve peace at home; the choice of aiding in the extermination of a lesser number of human beings in order that a greater number might be saved; the choice of remaining silent in the face of evil in order that some effectiveness for good might be continued in secret.

Such moral dilemmas are not unique to our time: what is unique is the capacity for evil possessed by those who posed them. Modern organizational forms and the advancements of technology have created a political potential that appears to pass beyond the measure of traditional ethical and legal judgments. When historians ponder the enormity of fascist offenses, they ponder the inadequacy of conventional Western values in an age of totalitarian politics and total war. "What meaning has the concept of murder," Hannah Arendt has asked, "when we are confronted with the mass production of corpses?" [1] And what meaning has the concept of guilt? What kind of moral and legal responsibility, for instance, should we attribute to the so-called "desk murderers" of the SS bureaucracy, men who administered a program of genocide, but who as individuals never killed anyone? No doubt too much of our ignorance about fascism has been concealed by an excessive emphasis on its irrationalism. Certainly it is no more irrational, as one writer has recently observed, to believe in the existence of a superior race than to believe in the equality of men. Yet historians should not be reluctant to admit that there are limits to their intellectual methods, and that there are things about the Nazis and their movement that no amount of further investigation will make more comprehensible. Our knowledge of what happened at Auschwitz has been vastly increased, but not our understanding. No doubt there is truth in a recent observation that the Nazi death camp will remain "the rock on which throughout eternity all rational explanations will crash and break apart." [2] Fascism thus leads the historian to the boundaries of human understanding and involves him in moral and legal questions for which his training has not prepared him.

But there are problems of a more practical sort as well. At one time, in an effort to assign specific meaning to the term "fascism," a number of writers sought to confine its use to Mussolini's movement in Italy. If others have not followed this example, it is because they thought they recognized similar "fascist" characteristics in other movements as well. At present, National Socialism in Germany has become, to an extent much greater than its Italian counterpart, the model for our mental conception of fascism. In Nazism, it has been asserted, fascism achieved its ideal form, a fascism emancipated from the restraints of conservative allies, rooted in favorable national soil, and possessed of sufficient material resources to pursue its deeper impulses. But it is possible as well

---

[1] Hannah Arendt, "The Concentration Camps," Partisan Review, July, 1948, p. 745.
[2] Emil L. Fackenheim, "Jewish Faith and the Holocaust," Commentary, August, 1968, p. 31.

to see it the other way around. Rather than being a fulfillment of fascist potentialities, Nazism instead could represent an aberration from fascist norms, a movement unique unto itself, *sui generis*, impelled to nihilistic extremes by the tormented mood of a nation in despair. In short, Nazism may distort our historical conception of European fascism rather than clarify it. "When we ask what there is in National Socialism that can be retained in a coherent definition of fascism," a French fascist has written, "the thing that strikes us is its alien character, that is to say its character of being fundamentally Germanic and unsuited to other peoples." [3]

Certainly without the Nazi experience fascism would have a decidedly different shape in our minds. It is not impossible to speak of a "good" fascism, a political ideal that sought to overcome the divisive effects of class hostility and partisan politics by forging an emotional bond of chauvinism and race, a movement that attempted to regenerate national energies by regimenting society like an army at the front. It should be remembered that in the years before the Axis alliance of 1936, fascist Italy was an accepted partner in the European balance of power. Mussolini's fascism could be integrated into the European community; Hitler's fascism blew the continent to pieces. Mussolini's fascism was full of the swagger and braggadocio familiar to Latin dictatorships; Hitler's fascism had a demonic and malignant quality that stirred revulsion among its enemies. So wicked did it appear to the eyes of civilized men, that even the Allied terror bombing of prostrate German cities seemed somehow consistent with mankind's struggle for decency and justice.

In the main the history of fascism has been written on evidence drawn from the German and Italian movements. The cautious student will be instructed by their differences as well as by their similarities, for fascism should not be understood as a singularly German or Italian experience: it was a European experience. Every nation contrived its own expression of the same phenomenon—different in style, different in the personality of leadership, but alike in a common quality that historians are wont to call "fascist."

Every fascist movement, of course, drew inspiration from the German and Italian models (and to that extent some degree of imitation was inevitable), but most had the ambition to create their own national version of the same thing. Nationalism was the common creed of all fascist organizations and therefore it must be expected that each would seek to express the uniqueness of its national traditions and symbols.

[3] Maurice Bardeche, *Qu' est-ce que le fascisme?* (Paris: Les Sept Couleurs, 1961), pp. 25–26.

For the historian, the task thus becomes to separate the "fascist" substance from the nationalist trappings. In this task, however, human limitations soon become apparent, for the demands of detailed historical research must necessarily restrict the number of fascist organizations that can be investigated with sufficient competence and depth. The result has been the formulation of general theories about fascism that have relevance only to a few of its specific forms. And such is the variety of fascism that evidence can be gathered to support theories that are themselves in conflict. Most theories therefore tend to stand or fall in accordance with the movement chosen to demonstrate them: what the study of one organization appears to prove, the study of another serves to deny. Indeed the more we learn of specifics, the less we understand in general. The facts and forms are abundant, but what in them is essentially "fascist"? It must be confessed that, in general, historians have agreed to use the term "fascism" without agreeing how to define it.

It is nevertheless essential for students of history to come to terms with fascism. For it must be recognized—disturbing as the thought may be—that fascism in Europe was not an historical accident. It was an authentic expression of the Western experience, an emergence of traditions and attitudes that had been nurtured in the innards of European society. Fascism must not be explained out of European history as an aberration; it must be explained into European history as an integral part of the continent's development. Santayana has remarked that not even God can change the past. If we are to understand our own history, we must try to understand fascism.

Some observers have argued that fascism should be understood as the politics of a civilization in crisis, the monstrous product of world war and social disintegration. But this begs the question. Why did the European crisis beget this kind of politics? Why fascism: why this kind of ideology, this kind of movement? And what is its relationship to the other political forces of the period? How are we to interpret its similarities with the communists on the left? How are we to explain its odd kinship with the conservatives on the right? What is the social nature of its political support? Why were its forces so weak and inconstant in England and France? Why were they so strong and fanatic in Germany? Are there fascist precedents in the past? And will there be a return of fascism in the future? Again these questions return us to our larger concern: what is the place of fascism in European history?

Not all scholars, of course, would agree that we have set the problem in proper perspective. Some would prefer a singularly national context, interpreting Nazism, for instance, as the logical result of the course of German history. Others propose a more universal conception, viewing fascism as a twentieth century expression of political experiences that have reoccurred throughout time. But many writers have been concerned from the beginning with the international and distinctly modern aspects of the movement and with the prospect that fascism revealed something fundamental about European society in our time. So contrary did it appear to Western traditions, so unforeseen was its arrival, and so extraordinary its outer appearance, that they immediately sought a deeper significance for its rise on the Continent. It appeared to them to have a meaning beyond itself: the study of fascism seemed a study in the existing condition of European civilization as a whole. The readings in this volume have been drawn from some of the most provocative works of these writers, men who seek the meaning of fascism through an understanding of its place in modern European history. If at times some of them devote primary attention to Germany and Italy, it is because the fascist parties in these countries were the most popular and influential, and therefore the most widely reported and researched. In weighing their conclusions, however, we must distinguish between what is uniquely fascist and what is uniquely German or Italian.

In the following remarks the views of these writers are divided into topical categories, but it should be admitted at the start that the arrangement is not always precise and orderly. The study of fascism has never been an exercise in bringing together opposing opinions, and even companionable views rest uneasily side by side. Conflicting interpretations have existed from the outset, shifting in emphasis as new evidence becomes available, and undergoing modification as the changing features of the present cast new light upon the past. If the earliest interpretations, written in the teeth of the emerging fascist movements, now appear inadequate and defective, it is in part because the movements themselves were transformed in the course of their existence. As they passed through changing experiences, they themselves underwent change. In the same way Europe—and Europe's position in the world—has changed since 1945, giving contemporary historians a different perspective on the fascist years. The result has been a continuing reassessment of fascism and its significance in European history. New efforts toward understanding have sought not only to correct past inaccuracies but to investigate unexplored dimensions, bringing new intellectual methods and the advantage of greater hindsight to the task of creating a more complete vision of the fascist experience. Thus our existing conceptions of fascism have evolved from a continuing study of our times. They are historical images that have not yet fully emerged from the historical process itself, and therefore carry the impressions of the period that produced them. In this sense the historiography of fascism should itself be understood historically. This volume is concerned not only with portraying the persistent intellectual controversy on fascism, but equally with tracing the important developments in the continuing scholarship on the subject, beginning with some of the most influential works of the 1930s and proceeding through to the major contributions of recent years.

FASCISM AS THE END OF LIBERAL SOCIETY

It was natural for the writers of the 1920s and 1930s to associate the rise of fascism with the momentous experiences of their times: the First World War, the postwar convulsions, the Bolshevik revolution, and the Great Depression. Deeply conscious of the connection between economic turmoil in Italy and Mussolini's "march on Rome" in 1922, and discerning a similar pattern in the sudden Nazi breakthrough during the depression years in Germany, many of them linked fascism to a crisis in Europe's capitalist economy. The writers in the first section of our volume are of very different opinions, but they share an agreement that fascism was related to a broader development of major historical importance—the breakdown of the social and economic order that had evolved out of the nineteenth century. It marked the *end of liberal society*, the passing of a social system characterized by uncontrolled capitalist competition and outmoded liberal ideas. Fascism, in their view, was politics in the wasteland: demagoguery to enthrall those who no longer could believe, terror to govern those who had lost respect for traditional authority, circuses for a society without enough bread. After all it was Mussolini himself who admitted that fascism arose in Italy without a program or doctrine. These writers were disposed to recognize the same intellectual poverty in every other fascist organization. All the ideological elements of the various movements—Italian corporatism, fascist "socialism," or Nazi racism—were for the most part regarded as sham and charlatanism, a kind of demagogic claptrap that had stirred the irresponsible impulses of unlettered peasants, unemployed workers, and insecure elements of the middle classes. In the works of these observers, fascism appears as a force both opportunist and unintelligent, a movement without ideas, without historic roots in the past, and without a utopian vision of the future.

Among the early critics of fascism, the Marxists were the first to develop a systematic conception of its place in European history. Inspired by Marx's own works on Bonapartism in France, they sought the meaning of Mussolini's dictatorship in its effects upon economic relationships and the class struggle. Other contemporaries interpreted the brutality and pagan ceremony of the Blackshirts as a belated out-cropping of barbarism, a momentary loss of mind and reason in a nation occasionally given to excesses of emotionalism and display. The Marxists however immediately examined the social significance of fascism's political style and revolutionary pretensions. Its revival of ancient Roman symbolism and imagery appeared to them to be less a restoration of past memories than a disguise for present ambitions. Proletarian revolutions, Marx had taught them, draw their inspiration from the future; reactionary ones conjure up "world-historical recollections in order to drug themselves concerning their own content." [4] Nor could they dismiss this first appearance of fascism as an isolated Italian phenomenon, an aberration from the historical direction of European development. What had happened in one part of the international capitalist system was potentially present in the system as a whole. Fascism was therefore an inherent possibility in all capitalist societies at the prevailing stage of economic development. Thus from Marxist preconceptions about the historical process emerged a recognition of fascism as an integral part of European history, a political expression of basic contradictions lying deeper in the social order.

In 1933, when Hitler's success in Germany turned the Communist Third International from thoughts of social revolution to preparations for a new party line of democratic defense against the fascist menace, a more or less official communist interpretation of the new political phenomenon was presented to the world Communist parties. Fascism, it was stressed, was a means of continuing the class relationships of the capitalist nations by undemocratic methods: the economic and social base remained the same, the political superstructure was changed to serve the needs of a class dictatorship. It was thus a product of bourgeois society in crisis, a last, desperate, authoritarian phase of capitalism. "Fascism," the International pronounced, "is the unconcealed, terroristic dictatorship of the most reactionary, chauvinistic, and imperialist elements of finance capital." [5]

The following year the British Communist R. Palme Dutt carried the message to English readers in his book *Fascism and Social Reform*, a work from which we have drawn our first reading selection. It should be indicated that Dutt's views—and more generally the Communist interpretation itself—are somewhat a conditioned response to the unexpected. We have already observed that nowhere in European literature

---

[4] Karl Marx, *The Eighteenth Brumaire of Louis Napoleon* (New York: International Publishers, n.d.), p. 16.

[5] Thirteenth Plenary Session of the Executive Committee of the Communist International, December, 1933.

—including Marxist literature—had the rise of fascism been foreseen. But what was especially disturbing to Marxists was the fact that the crisis of capitalism, which in a way fulfilled one part of Marx's prophecy, appeared to be producing fascism rather than socialism. Marxist scholars were confident in associating fascism with a breakdown in the international economic system, and certainly it was not difficult to discover financial connections between the fascists and a number (though a limited number) of business interests. Yet how were they to explain the strength and success of a reactionary movement enlisted in the defense of a doomed and disintegrating social order? The fascists themselves could easily enough be dismissed as agents of the bourgeoisie, but what accounted for their mass support in the populace, a support that extended into the ranks of peasants and workers? A movement which, in Marxist eyes, had been created to resist the emergence of the masses seemingly was winning the masses to its side. In this sense the rise of fascism revealed something about the condition of European socialism as well. Even in the midst of depression, unemployment, and soup lines, the parties of the left were losing the struggle for the minds of the popular classes. Thus in his evaluation of fascist success, Dutt necessarily attempts to account for the failure of his own movement: one was the measure of the other. Not unexpectedly—considering the polemics of the day—he discovers the cause in the "treason" and deception of the leaders of democratic socialism, men then considered the most dangerous among communism's enemies on the left. It was they, he argues, who turned the workers away from revolution, leaving them passive and confused before the terrorism and "social demagoguery" of the class enemy. The masses were not won to fascism; they were delivered over disillusioned and disarmed. The fascist conquest of power is achieved, Dutt concludes, "when the breakdown of the old capitalist institutions and the advance of the working-class movement have reached a point at which the working class should advance to the seizure of power, but when the working class is held in by reformist leadership."

Although this explanation conformed to Stalinist orthodoxy, it was not particularly convincing to those of other political persuasions. It faltered most seriously, some considered, in its refusal to recognize the authentic popular basis of fascism. Somehow the fascist movements provided an emotional satisfaction to compensate for the economic distress of the times. A proper understanding, a number of scholars concluded, necessarily required a psychological dimension. Certainly, they agreed, fascism could not be separated from the breakdown of existing society, but social breakdown has psychic implications. A socioeconomic analysis of capitalist disintegration—such as the Marxists proposed—was not enough to comprehend the historical appearance of fascism. It was also necessary to understand the resulting state of mind. In the century of Freud, and especially in the case of a movement which consciously directed its appeal to the emotional impulses of the "inner man," the study of politics in an age of crisis could not be separated from the study of human psychology.

The second reading combines the insights of psychology with the economic and social categories of Marxist historical analysis. It is drawn from a work that should be included in the intellectual formation of every undergraduate student: Erich Fromm's *Escape from Freedom*. A respected social psychologist, Fromm attempts to understand fascism (and specifically Nazism) as a reaction to the psychological stresses of modern monopoly capitalism. The fascist breakthrough, he believes, was prepared by a psychic malaise that spread through all social classes during the economic dislocations that followed the world war. Even the working class, the class whose organization and solidarity was most effective in withstanding the lure of fascism, eventually was overtaken by a mood of isolation and despair that sapped its will to resist. But more important was the willing flight toward fascism on the part of the lower middle class—that "forward-looking and backward-longing" class that figures so largely in nearly every analysis of fascist support. It is a class, Fromm contends, which in considerable measure possesses a unique "sadomasochistic" personality structure, a character formation which created a kind of Hitler within themselves. The result was an ambivalent passion for power and submission that sought fulfillment in fascism. For Fromm, who is himself a Marxist of democratic and humanist convictions, it was this popular mass support which was the most disturbing aspect of fascism. "We have been compelled to recognize," he observes, "that millions in Germany were as eager to surrender their freedom as their fathers were to fight for it; that instead of wanting freedom, they sought for ways of escape from it."

In the following selection, the conservative political economist Peter Drucker also traces the success of fascism to the condition of the European mind. But for him the roots of the problem lay not in the peculiar mental development of various social classes, but in a vaguely conscious intellectual crisis that was universal throughout society. The West, he contends in a brilliantly conceived argument, had arrived at the end of a belief that was once the underlying premise of all its social and political thought. In the mind of the nineteenth century, man was the creature of economic forces, a personality shaped by the pain and

pleasure of economic fortune, motivated by economic gain, and re-
warded by economic success. Out of this had come the great ideological
conceptions of our time, the Marxist vision of social justice through
new economic arrangements, the laissez-faire illusion of a free society
functioning around a free market, and the widespread popular belief
that human happiness could be achieved by a higher ordering of economic processes. Drucker insists, however, that with the coming of the
great catastrophes of the twentieth century, reason and meaning appeared to go out of the economic order: to the popular mind the world
of men and machines no longer functioned by logical design. Europeans,
he argues, were living through the death of "Economic Man." What
he means, put more precisely, is that they had lost faith in liberal and
socialist thought. The rise of fascism, Drucker concludes, marks the
disinheritance of the dominant economic ideologies of the nineteenth
century. At the end of their belief in economic reason, men were seeking
to restore the industrial process through fascist magic.

Each writer in this first section of our volume, it will be noticed, has
surveyed fascism from a different point on the political spectrum: Dutt
from the communist left, Fromm from the viewpoint of humanist socialism, and finally Drucker from the conservative right. To an extent
this has determined the direction and substance of their vision. Perhaps
inevitably each has incorporated into his descriptions the attitudes and
assumptions of his own political perspective—attitudes toward social
classes, the value of democratic opinion, and the historical process itself.
Moreover, each has involved himself in a causal analysis of fascism that
is at the same time a theoretical critique of European society between
the wars. Writing in a period when fascism was still undergoing change
and development, and when its outlines were largely unintelligible, the
authors sought to understand the movement through the historical conditions out of which it emerged. Sensing its roots in the deeper problems
of their time, and conscious of its identity with the desperate moods
produced by the Great War and the world depression, they defined fascism as a force arising out of a larger crisis of liberal society in the West.
We are therefore confronted with partisan interpretations of fascism
that in addition are partisan interpretations of the existing social order.
In fascism's coerciveness and ideological poverty the writers find the
reflection of a society at the end of its creative energies and intellectual
resources. The movement was not, to their minds, the shape of things
to come, but rather the evidence that something in the old system had
ended. Fascism was an escape from individual fears into collective
delusions, a change—as another scholar phrased it—from "unorganized

insecurity to organized insecurity." [6] But the underlying sources of social disintegration remained, awaiting the solution of more constructive and humane forces.

FASCISM AS TOTALITARIANISM

If these early interpretations of fascism were inspired by the condition of Europe in the 1920s and 1930s, those that came later were created from more monstrous visions. It was no longer the spectacle of marching men, mass rallies, and fascist street gangs that impressed itself upon the mind, but the dreadful images of mass murder and the Nazi state at war. Most early writers sought to understand Hitler's movement against the background of Mussolini's success in Italy; under the impact of later events other authorities were convinced that Stalin's regime in the Soviet Union provided a more meaningful comparison. Both systems had a monolithic and murderous quality that appeared more fundamental than their ideological differences. Nazism's evolution away from the background of the depression years and toward a seemingly heightened form of fascism, and its parallel development with Stalinism in the late 1930s, encouraged the notion that a proper understanding of the two antagonistic movements might really begin with a recognition of their inner connection. Their sudden embrace in the Hitler-Stalin pact of 1939 and the awesome sight of their mortal combat in World War II insured the continuation of such speculations into the postwar world, where the Soviet challenge in the cold war provided them with a special relevance and fascination for scholars in the United States.

Some scholars had already connected fascism and bolshevism in the 1920s, almost from the moment that the Blackshirts appeared on the Italian scene. Being for the most part men of liberal and democratic opinion, they associated Mussolini and the Bolsheviks with a common assault upon free institutions and open societies. It appeared to some of them that the terms "Left" and "Right"—descriptions which had never been very satisfactory anyway—no longer defined political reality, but rather seemed to obscure it. To interpret the fascists as a right-wing phenomenon, to seat them beside monarchists and reactionaries in parliaments, and to consider them a radical extension of diehard conservatism, was to be blind to the remarkable similarities between Mussolini and his communist "enemies." With the rise of fascism, it appeared, the heat and passion at both ends of the political spectrum had

[6] Karl Mannheim, *Man and Society in an Age of Reconstruction* (London: Kegan Paul, 1940), p. 135.

resulted in a fusion of the political extremes—the ends had met, completing the circle of political beliefs. Bolshevism was a fascism of the left, just as fascism was a bolshevism of the right.

From these beginnings an inquiry has gone forward into the underlying unity of radical movements. The result has been a continuing literature on the connections between the two political poles, with social scientists seeking the common roots of left and right extremism, and psychologists particularly involved in working out theoretical models of what has been called the "authoritarian personality." But it was the dual experience with Hitler and Stalin, much more than the earlier confrontation between fascism and communism in Italy, which gave these studies their real impetus and significance. Indeed the sight of the dictatorships in Berlin and Moscow evolving side by side has stimulated some of the most original political thought of our time. It has provided our mental imagery of the modern police state and revealed the existing possibilities for total power over men. The two regimes opened our vision into the world of 1984, and returned the concepts of mystery and evil to political theory. Fascism of course had always been identified with barbarity; but with Nazism, fascism became demonic, and the moral question became inseparable from its history. Together the Nazis and Stalinists accomplished the most colossal achievements and the greatest political crimes of the century: the Soviet Five Year Plans, the Nazi conquest of Europe, and the mass killings of the Great Purges and the "Final Solution." "In our world," Hannah Arendt has remarked on these episodes, "real events, real destinies, have long surpassed the wildest imagination of novelists."

For those writing in the years before Stalin's death in 1953, it was evident that such things had not ended with the Allied victory over Germany in 1945. Nazism had passed but the thing that it represented continued on. New systems were building in the recently established communist regimes of Asia and eastern Europe, and preparations for another round of political terror appeared to be going forward in the Soviet Union. Against this background of monolithic regimes a remarkable group of scholars fashioned an original and impressive interpretation of the new political forces. They themselves were part of a great immigration of intellectuals that came to America between the wars, some of them arriving as political refugees from the European dictatorships. As a generation of scholars they are now being recognized as one of the greatest influences in the recent intellectual history of the American nation. The political thinkers among them vastly enriched the study of political science in the United States, introducing a European dimension to American scholarship that deepened and matured our understanding of the great authoritarian systems of this century. For many of them the impressions of the twin evolution of Nazism and Soviet communism had been heightened by the intrusion of the regimes into their personal lives, and they brought to their subject a deep concern with the total claim upon the individual made by the two movements and with the resulting danger to the private existence of men.

From their own ideological development, a number of these thinkers had inherited the intellectual attitudes of east and central European conservatism, with its philosophical caste of mind, its pessimism toward the human condition in modern society, and its sensitivity to the residue of myth and superstition existing in the popular mind. Perhaps as a result, they sought the foundations of the new dictatorships in modernity itself. The things that liberal thinkers interpreted as the measure of human progress—science, industry, urban growth, and mass democracy—appeared to them as the very factors that made possible unprecedented forms of human oppression. From these factors, they believed, came the conditions necessary to the fulfillment of that urge toward totality which was inherent in modern secular ideologies: total dominion over things, total power over men, total control over the community. Where writers on the left identified fascism as undemocratic and reactionary, these scholars considered it to be a result of mass democracy in modern conditions. For them fascism and bolshevism together were part of the same mass contagion that endangered culture and civilization; both were expressions of that "revolt of the masses" which conservative thinkers had warned of at the beginning of the century. As a result of the involved interworkings of technology, mass society, and the pseudoscientific ideologies inherited from the past century, they concluded, a new and unique form of government had been created: totalitarianism.[7]

In our second group of readings, three prominent authorities of this important school of interpretation describe their conception of the totalitarian system. Carl Friedrich and Zbigniew Brzezinski in the first selection are concerned with its independent parts: the dictator, the party, the secret police, and the other features which make up their totalitarian model. However, it is not each of these things existing independently which is important, they insist, but all of them interworking together. The parts reinforce each other, quicken each other, drive each other toward further extremes. Together they form a whole greater

---

[7] The term "totalitarianism" is used here specifically in connection with the interpretation of this particular conservative school of thought. The word itself frequently is given a more common meaning and has earlier origins, being accepted by Mussolini himself to describe the fascist government in Italy as early as 1925.

than the sum of its parts, a machine progressively accelerated by the meshing of its components, a system of self-perpetuating energies, impelled toward a totality of power by the increasing momentum of its own operation. The result is a form of government characterized by an unstable synthesis of bureaucratic control and revolutionary dynamism, a government at one and the same time driven toward the absolute enforcement of order and the lawless undertaking of great historical tasks. It is both organized and shapeless, efficient in its surveillance over the human spirit and wasteful in its reckless consumption of men and resources. Whether run by fascists or communists, the operations of the system are basically the same: their tendency, in the opinion of the writers, is to become increasingly more oppressive and more "total." What is worse, they appear to be designed for survival into the future.

In the second selection Hannah Arendt finds the essential driving forces of the totalitarian system in ideology and terror. Fascist ideas, for the writers in the first section of this volume, were mostly wind and smoke; for Arendt, they are the higher impulse of the movement itself. In her opinion fascist racial theories were to the Nazi dictatorship what Marxist ideology was to the Soviet system: both prescribed the laws of a higher order of things that the regimes were inspired to impose upon mankind. It was this mission of preparing humanity to conform to the will of higher laws that propelled the systems against every trace of individual spontaneity and resistance and even against the independent existence of men themselves. The outcome, she argues, is total terror, "the essence of totalitarian government," the means by which all men become one mass, and in effect each man becomes superfluous. And because new human beings are born, the totalitarian mission remains always unfulfilled and terror becomes perpetual. Nazis and Stalinists reach their true end only in the concentration camp, the place where totalitarian society achieves its purest form.

This concept of totalitarianism, as it was fully developed in the 1950s, captured the imagination of the cold war generation. It was reassuring to the West to think that Hitler and Stalin were basically the same. Such comparisons gave meaning to the great power confrontation between the United States and the Soviet Union and provided ideological substance for the propaganda imagery of a "free world" set against a monolithic and aggressive empire of terrorized peoples and captive nations. In this construction of things, however, fascism had become subordinated to a larger concern with totalitarianism, within which fascism itself was merely a particular variation in form. Furthermore it was really Nazism, and not the other fascist movements, that was predominant in the mind of such scholars as Friedrich and Arendt. Certainly they drew upon fascist experiences elsewhere, but it was National Socialism in Germany that provided the necessary historical equivalent to Stalinism in the Soviet Union, and it was the comparative study of these two systems that inspired the outlines of the totalitarian model itself. Through an escalation of ideological concepts fascism became identified with Nazism, Nazism became identified with totalitarianism, and totalitarianism became identified with terror and concentration camps. Put more directly: fascism equalled mass murder.

Despite the political popularity of the totalitarianism interpretation during the 1950s, there were many scholars who denied its logic and relevance. Their disagreement was fundamental: Nazism and Stalinism, they insisted, were not the same, and it was wrong to associate one regime with the other. The identification of totalitarian movements with "the masses"—which in their opinion was more the result of conservative bias than impartial analysis—concealed the decisive differences in the social bases of fascism and communism. Objective investigation, they considered, had to return from the notion of "mass" to the concept of "class." Furthermore, it was superficial to compare the crude Nazi theories of race conflict with Marxism's sophisticated ideas of class struggle: one was not the intellectual equivalent of the other. The study of fascism, these scholars believed, had to be recovered from the abstractions of conservative political philosophy and the mythology of cold war propaganda. Their time would come in the 1960s when, with the easing tensions between East and West, the concept of totalitarianism appeared to lose the supporting evidence of contemporary events.

FASCISM AS A RADICAL FORM OF TRADITIONAL POLITICAL PROTEST

There had always existed a certain tension between the theory of totalitarianism and the realities of the world. The premise of Friedrich and Brzezinski that totalitarian dictatorship was "a logical extension of certain aspects of our modern industrial society" fit badly into the context of such nations as China, North Vietnam, and Albania, where regimes based on the Soviet model arose out of peasant societies. Totalitarianism, it would appear, was a singularly Western conception; but for a time cold war events in Europe made up for what was lacking in the theory in other parts of the world. The developing Soviet-American thaw of the late 1950s, however, combined with continuing news of changing events behind the "Iron Curtain," strengthened the suspicion that the theory itself was integrally related to cold war thinking in the West. Stalin's successors in the Kremlin were unmistakably dismantling the more oppressive machinery of the Soviet terror apparatus, Moscow's authority was eroding within the world Marxist movement, and the image of a monolithic communist bloc was giving way to new visions of "other roads toward socialism." Meanwhile a new generation of scholars in the West was beginning the "revision" of cold war historiography, seeking the origins of the conflict as much in the anticommunist intransigence of American policy as in the "totalitarian" character of the Soviet regime. In fine, the world that had inspired the theory of totalitarianism was passing into history, and with it passed many of the mental habits that determined its thinking.

With the early 1960s there was a developing intellectual inclination to consider that the cold war was over and that the West had passed through an extreme political crisis which had originated with the rise of fascism in the interwar years and climaxed with the death of Stalin in 1953. A new sense of historical periodization was emerging, an awareness that sometime in the 1950s the world had entered a new situation, and that we no longer lived in the era of the depression, the fascist dictators, and the Stalinist purges. That era of crisis was now a part of our past, and it was necessary to place it in perspective. Writers of the totalitarianism school had been concerned with what was novel and unique in the new dictatorships of the crisis period, a period which for them existed in the present. A number of writers in the 1960s became concerned instead with the period's continuity with the past. Their intent was to trace fascist ideas back into earlier intellectual developments and to discover how the heat of the crisis period had fired them into the radical ideologies of the fascist movements themselves. In the work of these writers, fascism was divorced from its totalitarian wedlock with communism and became identified as a *radical form of traditional political protest.*

Among these writers, the three American scholars presented in the third section of our volume particularly reveal the richness and variety of this attempt to discover the meaning of fascism in the perspective of European traditions. Together they are a study in unity and contrast, beginning in a common purpose to return the study of fascism to conventional political discourse, and ending in substantial disagreement among themselves. Where the totalitarianism school concluded that the appearance of a new phenomenon made necessary a new vocabulary to describe it, these writers adopted the standard political terminology of left, right, and center. Thus in the first selection Eugen Weber traces fascism to an ideological conjunction of right and left during the nineteenth century. In the following work, however, Seymour Lipset argues that it should properly be understood as an extremist movement of the political center. And finally John Weiss concludes that it is really a radical extension of the conservative right. Starting from common assumptions, the three men have finished by identifying fascism with every point on the political spectrum.

Among the three writers, Weber remains closest to the conceptions of the totalitarianism theory. Although he views fascist ideas in the longer perspective of European development, he nevertheless recognizes fascism itself as the unique creation of modern times, the result of a historic convergence of older ideological currents from the left and right to form a political force new and original to our times. For him fascism was an expression of modern attitudes, a twentieth-century assault upon nineteenth-century notions of man and society, a truly revolutionary movement drawing on collective sentiments that had spread through socialist and nationalist thought since the French Revolution. For Lipset and Weiss on the other hand, fascism was not an expression of the modern world, but a reaction against it. It was not modern, but antimodern, a political backlash against the advance of industrialization and social progress. Fascist ideas appear to them to be only radical extensions or vulgarizations of older arguments against the industrial state, the type of ideas that have always served the protests of certain social classes menaced by the modernization process.

With Lipset and Weiss, we have returned to the notion of fascism as a revolt of the middle and lower middle classes, the uprising of the unorganized against the organized, the protest of the "little man" against big business and big labor, against the state above and "social inferiors" below. Lipset associates fascist sentiment with the dark underside of middle class liberalism; it is to him a political agony of white collar workers and small entrepreneurs who in better circumstances supported the liberal center. For his part Weiss insists that such men ceased being liberals in the nineteenth century—or at least that they continued to be liberals "only in the sense that members of the John Birch Society are liberal." In reality, he contends, they evolved into a "radical Right," a new "ultraconservatism" which provided the political base for fascism. But this base of "little men," in his opinion, is not enough to understand fascism's success: the movement had its attractions for big men as well—landowners, industrialists, and military officers. For fascist propaganda was in part a plebeian version of traditional aristocratic notions of hierarchy and order and therefore had its appeal among the mighty as well as the helpless. Thus the fascist front, in his view, was in fact a conservative front, extending from the "revolutionary reactionaries" who marched with the fascist legions, through the "new conservatism" of the middle-class right, to the "traditional conservatism" of the upper classes. "Fascism, after all," he concludes, "is a conservative social movement, however radical."

At this point many readers no doubt will question whether the resort to traditional political concepts has made the phenomenon of fascism more understandable and whether Weiss's terms are not more appropriate to contemporary American politics than to European fascism between the wars. His arguments are valuable, however, in illustrating what can be called the liberal interpretation of fascism, the view that fascism was a reactionary protest against the democratic and industrial society that liberalism itself was creating. Fascism becomes here a movement of liberalism's historic political enemies. It is seen as an alliance of reactionaries and conservatives *in extremis*, a contemporary form of anti-liberalism made more malicious and savage by the quickening pace of modernization. The fascist mind, in this context, becomes identified with the intolerance and bigotry that liberals associate with the conservative mentality: the fear of social change, a contempt for intellectualism, and an instinctive opposition to all that is different, ambiguous, and complex. Although Weiss himself disputes the main liberal contention that fascism was a "revolt against reason," he makes it even more consistently a "revolt against liberalism," a "workable, if frightening, set of political, social, and economic alternatives to the reigning liberalism of the West."

The central thesis of the conservative writers of the totalitarianism school had been that fascism was a part of the revolt of the masses in modern society; the central thesis of liberal writers such as Weiss and Lipset is that it was the revolt of reactionary elements *against* modern society. Both views give evidence of the same thing: the tendency of scholars to interpret fascism in terms of their own political beliefs and to find in its sordid history the confirmation of their own opinions. This is perhaps not so much a political use of history as a political understanding of it. In either case, fascism is associated with the forces of the enemy and not with the forces within ourselves.

FASCISM AS A REVOLT AGAINST MODERNISM

Because Lipset and Weiss had connected fascism with a continuing political tradition from the European past, they recognized its potential to appear again at some point in the future. To their minds, however, it appeared likely that the future of fascism lay in the developing countries rather than the West. Lipset considered that "the well-to-do, highly industrialized and urbanized nations" had perhaps become resistant to extremist movements; and Weiss doubted the prospects for right-wing success in "liberalized-consensus societies." In these conclusions the two writers reflected an intellectual opinion that had been developing through the late fifties and middle sixties: the belief that with the passing of fascism and Stalinism the West had entered a period of relative political stability. It was a time—between the cold war and the present outbreak of student and radical unrest—when European political consciousness seemingly had achieved a higher sense of community, civility, and restraint. At the end of his important study on Western politics, Lipset affirmed that "the fundamental political problems of the industrial revolution have been solved," and that the left and right largely had resolved their murderous quarrels. Substantial agreement had been reached on the questions of the welfare state, the democratic process, and the nature of political institutions. As a result, he concluded, "serious ideological controversies have ended at home": Europe and America had arrived at "the end of ideology." [8]

The road to the modern world, it appears from these deductions, leads through class conflict and radical protest, but the higher stages of industrial growth somehow work to resolve the problems generated during the earlier phase. Modernization thus involves both a process and a consummation: societies undergoing industrial development are subject to seizures of political extremism; advanced industrial societies are characterized by political consensus. In this context fascism could be linked to a crisis period in the modernization process. It could be seen as a political radicalism associated with a particular level of European development, a radicalism which, once confronted and overcome, was unlikely to recur again in the West. In the final section of our volume, three scholars writing in the 1960s develop this conception further, identifying fascism as a *revolt against modernism*.

In the first selection, Barrington Moore echoes many of the liberal preconceptions about fascism, locating its roots in conservatism, and identifying it as an "ideology of the radical Right." He handles these familiar notions in an original and stimulating way, however, and makes the relationship between conservatism and fascism more subtle and involved than in earlier interpretations. More importantly he works

[8] *Political Man* (New York: Anchor Books, 1963), pp. 442, 445. The idea that the West had arrived at "the end of the ideological age" was first suggested by the French sociologist Raymond Aron in 1955. For its full development, see especially Daniel Bell, *The End of Ideology* (Glencoe, The Free Press, 1960).

together his conclusions into a remarkable survey of the modernization process as it has unfolded in world history. Moore's thoughts here must be understood within the wider context of historical developments in the postwar world: the evolution of a "postindustrial society" in Europe and America, the arrival of the Soviet Union as a great industrial power, and the political emergence of the "Third World." These developments, becoming fully conscious in the 1950s, motivated Western scholars to visualize the past development of their own nations against the background of Soviet industrialization and the developing economies of the nonindustrial world. The result was a new intellectual concern with modernization as a historical process, with the impetus and obstacles to industrialization, and with the use in historical analysis of economic theories of industrial growth.

For Moore, therefore, the study of fascism was part of a larger study of modernization. There were, in his view, several roads for nations to follow into the modern world: one led toward capitalist democracy, one toward communism, and another toward fascism. This last one, as he describes it, was the way of "conservative modernization from above," an attempt by conservative statesmen to create a modern state without sacrificing premodern values. It led in time to fascism, "an attempt to make reaction and conservatism popular and plebeian." Like other liberal scholars, Moore attributes an important role to the middle class in the rise of fascism, but his real concern is with the nobility and peasantry. It is the historical fate of these two preindustrial classes which, to his mind, determines the direction of a nation's path toward modernity. Where aristocratic attitudes have prevailed over bourgeois attitudes in the advance toward industrialization, and where they have continued to find response in the countryside, the way to fascism has been prepared. Certain inclinations toward fascism, Moore believes, may be present in every society undergoing the pressures of industrialization, but if fascism is to flourish and arouse popular support, it requires the preexistence of moods and attitudes that conservative modernization has prepared and preserved. In this way the history and geography of fascism —as well as its political intensity—have been determined: thus its radical expression in "Prussian" Germany where "conservative modernization" was furthest advanced; thus its strength in such "feudal" and traditionalist nations as Japan, Italy, and Spain; and thus its weakness in "bourgeois" France and middle-class England.

Elsewhere in his study, Moore attempts to connect fascism with a cultural and moral tradition leading back to the origins of conservative and reactionary mythology. We are accustomed of course to this propensity of liberal thinkers to find connections between fascism and conservatism, but Moore's thoughts on the matter are particularly suggestive and penetrating. Certainly it can be argued that an understanding of the cultural and moral content of fascism may be more vital to our comprehension of the fascist mentality than the conventional preoccupation with its barbarism and criminality. Indeed it is possible that a fundamental moral inspiration may have been at the very source of fascism's dark thoughts and brutal deeds. But what is essential for Moore in these cultural and moral values is that they are inherently at odds with the industrial condition. They are a residue of reactionary longings and premodern nostalgia, a complex of human irrationalities that—as he would like to believe—may be somehow "flushed down the drain of history" by the progressive advance of industry. In brief, if "conservative modernization" prepares the road toward fascism, industrialism hopefully prepares the way beyond it.

Others have ventured further in this direction. Concluding our volume, the historians Ernst Nolte and Wolfgang Sauer contend that the advance of modernism in Europe brought not only the passing of fascism on the Continent but its end as a significant movement in the world as a whole. Moore, in company with Lipset and Weiss, anticipated that the future of fascism lay in the emerging nations beyond Europe; Nolte and Sauer anticipate no future at all. Fascism, for them, was integrally related to European conditions and to the era of the two world wars: it was a movement unique in space and time, without precedent in the past and improbable again in the years ahead. It is because fascism is "dead," Nolte reveals, that its historical meaning can now be discovered.

Nolte's *Three Faces of Fascism* is perhaps the most important work on fascism yet written; it is also the most difficult and the most exciting. Certainly none of the summary remarks to be made here can do justice to the complexity of its arguments, nor can the excerpts in the readings reveal the sweep and depth of the author's vision. These appreciations must await the intellectual adventure of reading the book itself. The work is an attempt to reconstitute the unity of history and philosophy, to explain fascism's historical significance by piercing to its metaphysical core. When it is finished fascism has been given theoretical origins in a philosophical tradition and a place in the history of our century that the fascists themselves would hardly comprehend. For Nolte at once integrates fascism into the longer perspective of antimodernist thought and separates it out of the historical continuum as an elemental expression of a particular era—an emanation of the period of the two world wars, outside of which it has neither a place nor a meaning.

Critics have reacted impatiently toward Nolte's persistent quest for essences and ultimate meanings. And many have disliked his inclination to treat political movements as incarnated ideas, and to speculate upon the historical process without sufficient attention to the stuff from which it is made: the forces, facts, and events of economic and social reality. No doubt there are some students, however, who feel that the traditional approaches to fascism have themselves left something missing and that there is a certain inner dimension to fascism which is essential to its nature. It is this that Nolte is seeking. The element that is most fundamental to fascism, he believes, is also the element that is most inaccessible to common historical methods. Thus where the meaning of fascism is concerned, the normal rules of evidence should not limit the search for understanding. "No desire for scientific objectivity," he insists, "can absolve us from trying to answer the most urgent question of our time."

In the end Nolte discovers the hidden wellsprings of fascism in a metapolitical outlook which he terms "resistance to transcendence." His thoughts here can be understood only in the context of the full work, but he means in general a lurking, subterranean fear of modernism's inherent momentum toward universalism and the transformation of "natural" relationships—a fear of the inevitable disintegration of national communities, races, and cultures. This fear, Nolte explains, becomes increasingly self-conscious with the advance of modernism, manifesting itself concretely in the first fascist movements, and finally in a last desperate impulse toward a "final solution," that is, toward salvation of the threatened community by means of a total destruction of "the enemy." This final frenzy of course is Nazism, fascism in its most extreme form, a demonic movement of such revolting brutality that every other inhuman act in history pales by comparison. Nazism's appearance marks for Nolte the final "life-and-death struggle" of fascism, the ultimate expression of "resistance to transcendence" now fully conscious and fully armed. With its passing, he appears to believe, something went out of Europe: the old world reintegrated itself at a higher level, and regained the sense of limit and community that had been lost in the past century.

Wolfgang Sauer finds some of these ideas important and useful, but most of them merely exasperating. In the final essay he combines a critique of Nolte's methods and conclusions with a thoughtful interpretive analysis of his own, making use of economic development theory to fill out Nolte's abstract notion of an "era of fascism." To him the era of fascism was a time when "military desperadoes" thrown off by the First World War came together with elements of the lower middle class to form the base of the fascist movements. The first group of men were a kind of modern *condottieri*, soldiers made superfluous by mechanized mass warfare; the second were small folk faced with economic extinction in the transition from commercial capitalism to industrial capitalism. Fascism thus appears again as a reactionary struggle against modernization, a *revolt of the losers* in the historical evolution toward advanced forms of organization. It is therefore in part—and here Sauer arrives at similar conclusions with Moore and Lipset—a political movement ill-fated by its own nature; it is a radicalization of thought associated with a certain level of economic growth, and thus a form of protest against modernization that will be resolved by the further progress of modernization itself. For Marxist writers of the 1930s, the higher stages of capitalist growth produced fascism; for these modern liberals, the higher stages of capitalist growth open the way beyond it. Modernism, it may be deduced, has a convenient way of doing in its enemies.

In connecting fascism with the front-fighter bands from the First World War, and therefore with the epoch of the war itself, Sauer adds an important historical complement to the interpretations based on economic development theory. It was the war, he contends, that militarized European society and brutalized its politics, revealing as a result the fascist potential inherent in the existing conditions of industrialization. The fascist triumph was therefore the result of unique conditions in the historical and economic development of Europe, and, as such, is unlikely to recur again on the Continent or in the wider world. Sauer thus gives Nolte's concept of an "era of fascism" a more precise connection with the period of the world wars as well as with particular levels of industrial growth. His most significant contribution however is a reconsideration of the place of German National Socialism in the larger context of international fascism. We have already observed how some writers in the 1930s, watching the construction of Hitler's dictatorship, began to separate Nazism from other forms of fascism, and to consider it either as a movement unique unto itself or as a higher, more pure expression of the fascist ideal. For some, Nazism could be studied only in its own terms; for others, to study Nazism was to study fascism itself. Neither alternative, in Sauer's opinion, has led to understanding: studied in itself, Nazism calls into question our very capacity to understand. "We can work out explanatory theories," he attests, "but if we face the facts directly, all explanations appear weak."

If it is to be understood, Sauer believes, Nazism must be reintegrated into fascism. It must be worked back into an international context that will reveal its universal features and at the same time account for its particular radicalism and savagery. This objective, we will recognize, can not be considered a new one: it has concerned, in a less conscious and more general way, many of the writers in this volume. Sauer's achievement is to approach the problem directly and to bring to it the most recent historical research and the latest speculation on economic development theory. As a result he is able to work the speculations of earlier scholars into a more adequate and critical synthesis. Before he is finished, it will be observed, he has given at least passing thought to most of the issues involved in the previous studies. For one thing leads to another, and to seek the place of Nazism in international fascism leads almost inevitably to the larger problem which is our central concern: the place of fascism in European history.

In Greek mythology, the hero Perseus vows to deliver the head of Medusa, the terrible Gorgon monster with hair of twisting snakes. But merely to set eyes upon her would mean his fate, for so grotesque was her appearance that men at once were turned to stone. However the goddess of wisdom Pallas Athena armed Perseus with her own bright shield and instructed him to keep his eyes fixed upon it as he approached the monster, watching Medusa's reflection on its shining surface until he was close enough to strike with his sword. Perhaps there is a lesson in this for us as well. In a way Nazism exists in the popular mind as the face of fascism, and it too causes a revulsion that immobilizes those who look upon it. Certainly it is National Socialism that is really at the core of the moral problem discussed earlier in these remarks. If we are to strike off this Gorgon head—and thus be permitted to look upon fascism more dispassionately—perhaps we also must approach it indirectly, viewing its outlines from a different perspective.

Many of the writers reviewed here have worked at the problem in this way, interpreting Nazism not as *the* face of fascism, but as one of fascism's many faces. They have seen it as a peculiarly radical part of an international movement that must be understood as a whole. But how great is that whole? Where does fascism begin and end? Although the word "fascism" belongs to our century, it can be argued that the thing itself existed before the word. Certainly there were few ideas among the fascists that could not be found in political movements of the past century. "A political creed does not need a name to be a reality," one historian has written, "any more than a child requires baptism to exist." [9] Yet the writers here have claimed to find something uniquely modern—and often antimodern—in fascism; and no doubt it can be debated that if fascist ideas were not original, the fascists at least put them together in a new way. Certainly no one who knew of

[9] Michael Hurst, "What is Fascism?" *The Historical Journal*, XI, no. 1 (1968): 168.

the ideas earlier could suspect that they would lead to the things that they did. We can recall again the opening line of this essay: "Fascism was the great political surprise of the first half of the twentieth century." No one had imagined it, anticipated it, or warned of its coming. This is a way of saying that fascism was inconceivable outside of our own century. But what is its meaning within our time? These remarks have only introduced this question. The following readings are concerned with providing an answer.

FASCISM AS THE END OF LIBERAL SOCIETY

R. Palme Dutt

FASCISM AS THE DICTATORSHIP OF DECAYING CAPITALISM

Rajani Palme Dutt, the son of an Indian physician residing in England, was born at Cambridge in 1896. He was expelled from Oxford University in 1917 for disseminating Marxist propaganda and went on to become a significant figure in the British Communist party. In 1962, Dutt received an honorary degree in history from Moscow University, in recognition of a lifetime of dedication to the intellectual life of British communism.

Fascism . . . is no peculiar, independent doctrine and system arising in opposition to existing capitalist society. Fascism, on the contrary, is the most complete and consistent working out, in certain conditions of extreme decay, of the most typical tendencies and policies of modern capitalism.

What are these characteristics which are common, subject to a difference in degree, to all modern capitalism and to fascism? The most outstanding of these characteristics may be summarized as follows:

1. The basic aim of the maintenance of capitalism in the face of the revolution which the advance of productive technique and of class antagonisms threatens.

From R. Palme Dutt, Fascism and Social Revolution (London, 1934), pp. 72–76, 80–82, 88–89, 177–78, 184. By permission of Lawrence and Wishart Limited. With certain exceptions, the readings in this book are reprinted without the footnotes which are present in the original publications.

2. The consequent intensification of the capitalist dictatorship.

3. The limitation and repression of the independent working-class movement, and building up of a system of organised class-cooperation.

4. The revolt against, and increasing supersession of, parliamentary democracy.

5. The extending state monopolist organisation of industry and finance.

6. The closer concentration of each imperialist bloc into a single economic-political unit.

7. The advance to war as the necessary accompaniment of the increasing imperialist antagonisms.

All these characteristics are typical, in greater or lesser degree, of all modern capitalist states, no less than of the specifically fascist states.

In this wider sense it is possible to speak of the development towards fascism of all modern capitalist states. The examples of the Roosevelt and Brüning regimes offer particular illustrations of near-fascist or pre-fascist stages of development towards complete fascism within the shell of the old forms. Nor is it necessarily the case that the development to fascism takes the same form in detail in each country.

The sum total of the policies of modern capitalism provide already in essence and in germ the sum total of the policies of fascism. But they are not yet complete fascism. The completed fascist dictatorship is still only so far realized over a limited area. What is the specific character of complete fascism? The specific character of complete fascism lies in the *means* adopted towards the realization of these policies, in the new *social and political mechanism* built up for their realization.

This is the specific or narrower significance of fascism in the sense of the fascist movements or the completed fascist dictatorships as realized in Italy, Germany, and other countries. Fascism in this specific or narrower sense is marked by definite familiar characteristics: in the case of the fascist movements, by the characteristics of terrorism, extralegal fighting formations, antiparliamentarism, national and social demagogy, etc.; in the case of the completed fascist dictatorships, by the suppression of all other parties and organizations, and in particular the violent suppression of all independent working-class organization, the reign of terror, the "totalitarian" state, etc.

It is to this specific sense of fascism, that is to say, to fully complete fascism, that we now need to come.

THE CLASS CONTENT OF FASCISM

What, then, is fascism in this specific or narrower sense?

The definitions of fascism abound, and are marked by the greatest diversity and even contradictory character, despite the identity of the concrete reality which it is attempted to describe.

Fascism, in the view of the fascists themselves, is a spiritual reality. It is described by them in terms of ideology. It represents the principle of "duty," of "order," of "authority," of "the state," of "the nation," of "history," etc. . . .

In the first place, all these abstract general conceptions which are paraded as the peculiar outlook of fascism have no distinctive character whatever, but are common to a thousand schools of bourgeois political philosophy, which are not yet fascist, and in particular to all national-conservative schools. The generalizations of "duty of cooperation," "duty towards others," "life as duty and struggle," "a high conception of citizenship," "the state above classes," "the common interest before self" . . . are the dreary commonplaces of all bourgeois politicians and petty moralizers to cover the realities of class domination and class exploitation. The professedly distinctive philosophy of the idealization of the state as an "absolute end" transcending all individuals and sections is only the vulgarization of the whole school of Hegel and his successors, constituting the foundation of the dominant school of bourgeois political philosophy. In all these conceptions there is not a trace of original or distinctive thought.

In the second place, it is in fact incorrect to look for an explanation of fascism in terms of a particular theory, in ideological terms. Fascism, as its leaders are frequently fond of insisting, developed as a movement in practice without a theory ("In the now distant March of 1919," says Mussolini in his Encyclopædia article, "since the creation of the Fascist Revolutionary Party, which took place in the January of 1915, I had no specific doctrinal attitude in my mind."), and only later endeavored to invent a theory in order to justify its existence. Fascism, in fact, developed as a movement in practice, in the conditions of threatening proletarian revolution, as a counterrevolutionary mass movement supported by the bourgeoisie, employing weapons of mixed social demagogy and terrorism to defeat the revolution and build up a strengthened capitalist state dictatorship; and only later endeavored to adorn and rationalize this process with a "theory." It is in this actual historical process that the reality of fascism must be found, and not in the secondary derivative attempts *post festum* at adornment with a theory. . . .

Wherein, then, lies the specific character of fascism?

The specific character of fascism cannot be defined in terms of abstract ideology or political first principles.

The specific character of fascism can only be defined by laying bare its *class basis*, the system of *class relations* within which it develops and functions, and the *class role* which it performs. Only so can fascism be seen in its concrete reality, corresponding to a given historical stage of capitalist development and decay. . . .

Fascism, although in the early stages making a show of vague and patently disingenuous anticapitalist propaganda to attract mass support, is from the outset fostered, nourished, maintained, and subsidized by the big bourgeoisie, by the big landlords, financiers, and industrialists.

Further, fascism is only enabled to grow, and is saved from being wiped out in the early stages by the working-class movement, solely through the direct protection of the bourgeois dictatorship. Fascism is able to count on the assistance of the greater part of the state forces, of the higher army staffs, of the police authorities, and of the lawcourts and magistracy, who exert all their force to crush working-class opposition, while treating fascist illegality with open connivance. . . .

Finally, has fascism "conquered power" from the bourgeois state dictatorship? Fascism has never "conquered power" in any country. In every case fascism has been placed in power from above by the bourgeois dictatorship. In Italy fascism was placed in power by the king, who refused to sign the decree of martial law against it, and invited Mussolini to power; Mussolini's legendary "March on Rome" took place in a Wagon-Lit sleeping car. In Germany fascism was placed in power by the president, at a time when it was heavily sinking in support in the country, as shown by the elections.

The bourgeoisie, in fact, has in practice passed power from one hand to the other, and called it a "revolution," while the only reality has been the intensified oppression of the working class.

After the establishment of the full fascist dictatorship, the policy has been still more openly and completely, despite a show of a few gestures of assistance to small capital, the most unlimited and ruthless policy of monopolist capital, with the whole machinery of fascism mercilessly turned against those of its former supporters who have been innocent enough to expect some anticapitalist action and called for a "second revolution."

Fascism, in short, is a movement of mixed elements, dominantly petit-bourgeois, but also slum-proletarian and demoralized working class, financed and directed by finance-capital, by the big industrialists, landlords and financiers, to defeat the working-class revolution and smash the working-class organizations. . . .

Where the majority of the working class has followed the line of Reformism (Germany, Italy, etc.), there at a certain stage fascism invariably grows and conquers.

What is the character of that stage? That stage arises when the breakdown of the old capitalist institutions and the advance of working-class movement has reached a point at which the working class should advance to the seizure of power, but when the working class is held in by reformist leadership.

In that case, owing to the failure of decisive working-class leadership to rally all discontented strata, the discredited old regime is able to draw to its support under specious quasirevolutionary slogans all the wavering elements, petit-bourgeoisie, backward workers, etc., and on the very basis of the crisis and discontent which should have given allies to the revolution, build up the forces of reaction in the form of fascism. The continued hesitation and retreat of the reformist working-class leadership at each point . . . encourages the growth of fascism. On this basis fascism is able finally to step in and seize the reins, not through its own strength, but through the failure of working-class leadership. The collapse of bourgeois democracy is succeeded, not by the advance to proletarian democracy, but by the regression to fascist dictatorship.

We are now in a position to reach our general definition of the character of fascism, the conditions of its development and its class rule. This definition has received its most complete scientific expression in the Programme of the Communist International in 1928:

Under certain special historical conditions the progress of the bourgeois, imperialist, reactionary offensive assumes the form of fascism.

These conditions are: instability of capitalist relationships; the existence of considerable declassed social elements, the pauperization of broad strata of the urban petit-bourgeoisie and of the intelligentsia; discontent among the rural petit-bourgeoisie, and, finally, the constant menace of mass proletarian action. In order to stabilize and perpetuate its rule the bourgeoisie is compelled to an increasing degree to abandon the parliamentary system in favor of the fascist system, which is independent of interparty arrangements and combinations.

The fascist system is a system of direct dictatorship, ideologically masked by the "national idea" and representation of the "professions" (in reality, representation of the various groups of the ruling class). It is a system that resorts to a peculiar form of social demagogy (anti-Semitism, occasional sorties against usurer's capital, and gestures of impatience with the parliamentary "talking shop") in order to utilize the discontent of the petit-bourgeois, the intellectual, and other strata of society; and to corruption through the building up of a compact and well-paid hierarchy of fascist units, a party apparatus and a bureaucracy. At the same time, fascism strives to permeate the working class by recruiting the most backward strata of the workers to its ranks, by playing upon their discontent, by taking advantage of the inaction of Social Democracy, etc.

The principal aim of fascism is to destroy the revolutionary labor vanguard, i.e., the communist sections and leading units of the proletariat. The combination of social demagogy, corruption and active White terror, in conjunction with extreme imperialist aggression in the sphere of foreign politics, are the characteristic features of fascism. In periods of acute crisis for the bourgeoisie, fascism resorts to anticapitalist phraseology, but, after it has established itself at the helm of state, it casts aside its anticapitalist rattle, and discloses itself as a terrorist dictatorship of big capital. . . .

IS THERE A "THEORY" OF FASCISM?

The first illusion that requires to be cleared out of the way is the illusion that there is a "theory" of fascism, in the same sense that there is a theory of liberalism, conservatism, communism, etc.

Many intellectuals, while "deploring" the "excesses" of fascism, allow themselves to be fascinated and drawn into elaborate speculative discussion of the "philosophy" of fascism—and are soon lost in the Serbonian bog of alternating "socialism," capitalism, corporatism, strongman worship, high moral adjurations and platitudes, antialien agitation, appeals to "unity," glorifications of war, torture-gloating, deification of primitive man, denunciations of big business, idolization of captains of industry, kicking of the dead corpse of the nineteenth century and "liberal-democratic humanitarian superstitions," exhumation of the considerably more putrescent corpses of mercantilism, absolutism, inquisitorial methods and caste-conceptions, racial theories of the inferiority of all other human beings save the speaker's own tribe, anti-Semitism, Nordicism, and all the rest of it.

The innocent may solemnly and painstakingly discuss at face value these miscellaneous "theories" provided to suit all tastes. But in fact their importance is rather as symptoms and by-products of the real system and basis of fascism than as its origin and raison d'être. The reality of fascism is the violent attempt of decaying capitalism to defeat the proletarian revolution and forcibly arrest the growing contradictions of its whole development. All the rest is decoration and stageplay, whether conscious or unconscious, to cover and make presentable or attractive ing its purpose. . . .

The whole outlook and ideology of fascism is in short nothing but a ragbag of borrowings from every source to cover the realities and practice of modern monopolist capitalism in the period of crisis and of extreme class war. There is not a single creative idea. Capitalism in its time, in its early progressive days, achieved a great constructive work, and carried enormously forward the whole of human culture in every field. The French Revolution spread a new life and a new understanding throughout the world, the outcome of which we can today be proud to inherit, even though we are today able to understand that its bourgeois basis inevitably set a limit to what it could achieve. The Russian Revolution opened a new era on a scale exceeding every previous change in human history, the full extent of which is still only beginning to be realized. But fascism has produced nothing, and can produce nothing. For fascism is the expression only of disease and death.

Erich Fromm

FASCISM AS LOWER-MIDDLE-CLASS PSYCHOLOGY

Erich Fromm (b. Frankfurt, Germany, 1900) taught and practiced in the field of psychoanalysis during the crisis years of the Weimar Republic. His early involvement in the mental problems of an eroding democratic society perhaps was decisive in shaping his later thought. With the Nazi victory, Fromm migrated to the United States where his reflections on the "escape from freedom" in his homeland were developed into a broad interpretation of the human condition in Western capitalist society.

This book is part of a broad study concerning the character structure of modern man and the problems of the interaction between psychological and sociological factors which I have been working on for several years and completion of which would have taken considerably longer. Present political developments and the dangers which they imply for the greatest achievements of modern culture—individuality and uniqueness of personality—made me decide to interrupt the work on the larger study and concentrate on one aspect of it which is crucial for the cultural and social crisis of our day: the meaning of freedom for modern man. . . .

It is the thesis of this book that modern man, freed from the bonds of preindividualistic society, which simultaneously gave him security and limited him, has not gained freedom in the positive sense of the realization of his individual self; that is, the expression of his intellectual, emotional and sensuous potentialities. Freedom, though it has brought him independence and rationality, has made him isolated and, thereby, anxious and powerless. This isolation is unbearable and the alternatives he is confronted with are either to escape from the burden of this freedom into new dependencies and submission, or to advance to the full realization of positive freedom which is based upon the uniqueness and individuality of man.

Modern European and American history is centered around the effort to gain freedom from the political, economic, and spiritual shackles that have bound men. . . .

Despite many reverses, freedom has won battles. Many died in those battles in the conviction that to die in the struggle against oppression was better than to live without freedom. Such a death was the utmost assertion of their individuality. History seemed to be proving that it was possible for man to govern himself, to make decisions for himself, and to think and feel as he saw fit. The full expression of man's potentialities seemed to be the goal toward which social development was rapidly approaching. The principles of economic liberalism, political democracy, religious autonomy, and individualism in personal life, gave expression to the longing for freedom, and at the same time seemed to bring mankind nearer to its realization. One tie after another was severed. Man had overthrown the domination of nature and made himself her master; he had overthrown the domination of the Church and the domination of the absolutist state. The *abolition of external domination* seemed to be not only a necessary but also a sufficient condition to attain the cherished goal: freedom of the individual.

The [First] World War was regarded by many as the final struggle and its conclusion the ultimate victory for freedom. Existing democracies appeared strengthened, and new ones replaced old monarchies. But only a few years elapsed before new systems emerged which denied everything that men believed they had won in centuries of struggle. For the essence of these new systems, which effectively took command of man's entire social and personal life, was the submission of all but a handful of men to an authority over which they had no control.

At first many found comfort in the thought that the victory of the authoritarian system was due to the madness of a few individuals and that their madness would lead to their downfall in due time. Others smugly believed that the Italian people, or the Germans, were lacking in a sufficiently long period of training in democracy, and that therefore one could wait complacently until they had reached the political maturity of the Western democracies. Another common illusion, perhaps the most dangerous of all, was that men like Hitler had gained power over the vast apparatus of the state through nothing but cunning and trickery, that they and their satellites ruled merely by sheer force; that the whole population was only the will-less object of betrayal and terror.

In the years that have elapsed since, the fallacy of these arguments has become apparent. We have been compelled to recognize that millions in Germany were as eager to surrender their freedom as their fathers were to fight for it; that instead of wanting freedom, they sought for ways of escape from it; that other millions were indifferent and did not believe the defense of freedom to be worth fighting and dying for. We also recognize that the crisis of democracy is not a peculiarly Italian or German problem, but one confronting every modern state. Nor does it matter which symbols the enemies of human freedom choose: freedom is not less endangered if attacked in the name of antifascism or in that of outright fascism.[1] This truth has been so forcefully formulated by John Dewey that I express the thought in his words: "The serious threat to our democracy," he says, "is not the existence of foreign totalitarian states. It is the existence without our own personal attitudes and within our own institutions of conditions which have given a victory to external authority, discipline, uniformity and dependence upon The Leader in foreign countries. The battlefield is also accordingly here—within ourselves and our institutions."

If we want to fight fascism we must understand it. . . .

Analysis of the human aspect of freedom and of authoritarianism forces us to consider a general problem, namely, that of the role which psychological factors play as active forces in the social process; and this eventually leads to the problem of the interaction of psychological, economic, and ideological factors in the social process. Any attempt to understand the attraction which fascism exercises upon great nations compels us to recognize the role of psychological factors. For we are dealing here with a political system which, essentially, does not appeal to rational forces of self-interest, but which arouses and mobilizes diabolical forces in man which we had believed to be nonexistent, or at least to have died out long ago. . . .

The physiologically conditioned needs are not the only imperative part of man's nature. There is another part just as compelling, one which is not rooted in bodily processes but in the very essence of the human mode and practice of life: the need to be related to the world outside oneself, the need to avoid aloneness. To feel completely alone

---

[1] I use the term fascism or authoritarianism to denote a dictatorial system of the type of the German or Italian one. If I mean the German system in particular, I shall call it Nazism.

and isolated leads to mental disintegration just as physical starvation leads to death. This relatedness to others is not identical with physical contact. An individual may be alone in a physical sense for many years and yet he may be related to ideas, values, or at least social patterns that give him a feeling of communion and "belonging." On the other hand, he may live among people and yet be overcome with an utter feeling of isolation, the outcome of which, if it transcends a certain limit, is the state of insanity which schizophrenic disturbances represent. This lack of relatedness to values, symbols, patterns, we may call moral aloneness and state that moral aloneness is as intolerable as the physical aloneness, or rather that physical aloneness becomes unbearable only if it implies also moral aloneness. . . .

II

The social history of man started with his emerging from a state of oneness with the natural world to an awareness of himself as an entity separate from surrounding nature and men. Yet this awareness remained very dim over long periods of history. The individual continued to be closely tied to the natural and social world from which he emerged; while being partly aware of himself as a separate entity, he felt also part of the world around him. The growing process of the emergence of the individual from his original ties, a process which we may call "individuation," seems to have reached its peak in modern history in the centuries between the Reformation and the present. . . .

What Protestantism had started to do in freeing man spiritually, capitalism continued to do mentally, socially, and politically. Economic freedom was the basis of this development, the middle class was its champion. The individual was no longer bound by a fixed social system, based on tradition and with a comparatively small margin for personal advancement beyond the traditional limits. He was allowed and expected to succeed in personal economic gains as far as his diligence, intelligence, courage, thrift, or luck would lead him. His was the chance of success, his was the risk to lose and to be one of those killed or wounded in the fierce economic battle in which each one fought against everybody else. Under the feudal system the limits of his life expansion had been laid out before he was born; but under the capitalistic system the individual, particularly the member of the middle class, had a chance —in spite of many limitations—to succeed on the basis of his own

merits and actions. He saw a goal before his eyes toward which he could
strive and which he often had a good chance to attain. He learned to
rely on himself, to make responsible decisions, to give up both soothing
and terrifying superstitions. Man became increasingly free from the
bondage of nature; he mastered natural forces to a degree unheard and
undreamed of in previous history. Men became equal; differences of
caste and religion, which once had been natural boundaries blocking the
unification of the human race, disappeared, and men learned to recognize each other as human beings. The world became increasingly free
from mystifying elements; man began to see himself objectively and
with fewer and fewer illusions. Politically freedom grew too. On the
strength of its economic position the rising middle class could conquer
political power and the newly won political power created increased possibilities for economic progress. The great revolutions in England and
France and the fight for American independence are the milestones
marking this development. The peak in the evolution of freedom in the
political sphere was the modern democratic state based on the principle
of equality of all men and the equal right of everybody to share in the
government by representatives of his own choosing. Each one was supposed to be able to act according to his own interest and at the same
time with a view to the common welfare of the nation.

In one word, capitalism not only freed man from traditional bonds,
but it also contributed tremendously to the increasing of positive freedom, to the growth of an active, critical, responsible self.

However, while this was one effect capitalism had on the process of
growing freedom, at the same time it made the individual more alone
and isolated and imbued him with a feeling of insignificance and powerlessness. . . .

The most important factor in this development is the increasing
power of monopolistic capital. The concentration of capital (not of
wealth) in certain sectors of our economic system restricted the possibilities for the success of individual initiative, courage, and intelligence.
In those sectors in which monopolistic capital has won its victories the
economic independence of many has been destroyed. For those who
struggle on, especially for a large part of the middle class, the fight assumes the character of a battle against such odds that the feeling of
confidence in personal initiative and courage is replaced by a feeling of
powerlessness and hopelessness. An enormous though secret power
over the whole of society is exercised by a small group, on the decisions
of which depends the fate of a large part of society. The inflation in

Germany, 1923, or the American crash, 1929, increased the feeling of insecurity and shattered for many the hope of getting ahead by one's own efforts and the traditional belief in the unlimited possibilities of success. . . .

Other factors have added to the growing powerlessness of the individual. The economic and political scene is more complex and vaster than it used to be; the individual has less ability to look through it. The threats which he is confronted with have grown in dimensions too. A structural unemployment of many millions has increased the sense of insecurity. . . .

The threat of war has also added to the feeling of individual powerlessness. To be sure, there were wars in the nineteenth century too. But since the last war the possibilities of destruction have increased so tremendously—the range of people to be affected by war has grown to such an extent as to comprise everybody without any exception—that the threat of war has become a nightmare which, though it may not be conscious to many people before their nation is actually involved in the war, has overshadowed their lives and increased their feeling of fright and individual powerlessness.

The "style" of the whole period corresponds to the picture I have sketched. Vastness of cities in which the individual is lost, buildings that are as high as mountains, constant acoustic bombardment by the radio, big headlines changing three times a day and leaving one no choice to decide what is important, . . . the beating rhythm of jazz— these and many other details are expressions of a constellation in which the individual is confronted by uncontrollable dimensions in comparison with which he is a small particle. . . .

III

We have brought our discussion up to the present period and would now proceed to discuss the psychological significance of fascism and the meaning of freedom in the authoritarian systems. . . .

Once the primary bonds which gave security to the individual are severed, once the individual faces the world outside of himself as a completely separate entity, two courses are open to him since he has to overcome the unbearable state of powerlessness and aloneness. By one course he can progress to "positive freedom"; he can relate himself spontaneously to the world in love and work, in the genuine expression of his emotional, sensuous, and intellectual capacities; he can thus become one again with man, nature, and himself, without giving up the independence and integrity of his individual self. The other course open to him is to fall back, to give up his freedom, and to try to overcome his aloneness by eliminating the gap that has arisen between his individual self and the world. This second course never reunites him with the world in the way he was related to it before he merged as an "individual," for the fact of his separateness cannot be reversed; it is an escape from an unbearable situation which would make life impossible if it were prolonged. This course of escape, therefore, is characterized by its compulsive character, like every escape from threatening panic; it is also characterized by the more or less complete surrender of individuality and the integrity of the self.

The first mechanism of escape from freedom I am going to deal with is the tendency to give up the independence of one's own individual self and to fuse one's self with somebody or something outside of oneself in order to acquire the strength which the individual self is lacking. Or, to put it in different words, to seek for new, "secondary bonds" as a substitute for the primary bonds which have been lost.

The more distinct forms of this mechanism are to be found in the striving for submission and domination, or, as we would rather put it, in the masochistic and sadistic strivings as they exist in varying degrees in normal and neurotic persons respectively. . . .

Although the character of persons in whom sadomasochistic drives are dominant can be characterized as sadomasochistic, such persons are not necessarily neurotic. It depends to a large extent on the particular tasks people have to fulfill in their social situation and what patterns of feelings and behavior are present in their culture whether or not a particular kind of character structure is "neurotic" or "normal." As a matter of fact, for great parts of the lower middle class in Germany and other European countries, the sadomasochistic character is typical, and, as will be shown later, it is this kind of character structure to which Nazi ideology had its strongest appeal. Since the term "sadomasochistic" is associated with ideas of perversion and neurosis, I prefer to speak of the sadomasochistic character, especially when not the neurotic but the normal person is meant, as the *authoritarian character.* This terminology is justifiable because the sadomasochistic person is always characterized by his attitude toward authority. He admires authority and tends to submit to it, but at the same time he wants to be an authority himself and have others submit to him. There is an additional reason for choosing this term. The fascist system call themselves authoritarian because of the dominant role of authority in their social and political structure. By the term "authoritarian character," we imply that it represents the personality structure which is the human basis of fascism. . . .

. . . For the authoritarian character there exist, so to speak, two sexes: the powerful ones and the powerless ones. His love, admiration and readiness for submission are automatically aroused by power, whether of a person or of an institution. Power fascinates him not for any values for which a specific power may stand, but just because it is power. Just as his "love" is automatically aroused by power, so powerless people or institutions automatically arouse his contempt. The very sight of a powerless person makes him want to attack, dominate, humiliate him. Whereas a different kind of character is appalled by the idea of attacking one who is helpless, the authoritarian character feels the more aroused the more helpless his object has become. . . .

In discussing the psychology of Nazism we have first to consider a preliminary question—the relevance of psychological factors in the understanding of Nazism. In the scientific and still more so in the popular discussion of Nazism, two opposite views are frequently presented: the first, that psychology offers no explanation of an economic and political phenomenon like fascism, the second, that fascism is wholly a psychological problem.

The first view looks upon Nazism either as the outcome of an exclusively economic dynamism—of the expansive tendencies of German imperialism, or as an essentially political phenomenon—the conquest of the state by one political party backed by industrialists and Junkers; in short, the victory of Nazism is looked upon as the result of a minority's trickery and coercion of the majority of the population.

The second view, on the other hand, maintains that Nazism can be explained only in terms of psychology, or rather in those of psychopathology. Hitler is looked upon as a madman or as a "neurotic," and his followers as equally mad and mentally unbalanced. According to this explanation, as expounded by L. Mumford, the true sources of fascism are to be found "in the human soul, *not in economics.*" He goes on: "In overwhelming pride, delight in cruelty, neurotic disintegration—in this and not in the Treaty of Versailles or in the incompetence of the German Republic lies the explanation of fascism."

In our opinion none of these explanations which emphasize political and economic factors to the exclusion of psychological ones—or vice versa—is correct. Nazism is a psychological problem, but the psychological factors themselves have to be understood as being molded by socioeconomic factors; Nazism is an economic and political problem, but the hold it has over a whole people has to be understood on psychological grounds. What we are concerned with in this chapter is this psychological aspect of Nazism, its human basis. This suggests two problems: the character structure of those people to whom it appealed, and the psychological characteristics of the ideology that made it such an effective instrument with regard to those very people.

In considering the psychological basis for the success of Nazism this differentiation has to be made at the outset: one part of the population bowed to the Nazi regime without any strong resistance, but also without becoming admirers of the Nazi ideology and political practice. Another part was deeply attracted to the new ideology and fanatically attached to those who proclaimed it. The first group consisted mainly of the working class and the liberal and Catholic bourgeoisie. In spite of an excellent organization, especially among the working class, these groups, although continuously hostile to Nazism from its beginning up to 1933, did not show the inner resistance one might have expected as the outcome of their political convictions. Their will to resist collapsed quickly and since then they have caused little difficulty for the regime (excepting, of course, the small minority which has fought heroically against Nazism during all these years). Psychologically, this readiness to submit to the Nazi regime seems to be due mainly to a state of inner tiredness and resignation, which . . . is characteristic of the individual in the present era even in democratic countries. . . .

An additional incentive for the loyalty of the majority of the population to the Nazi government became effective after Hitler came into power. For millions of people Hitler's government then became identical with "Germany." Once he held the power of government, fighting him implied shutting oneself out of the community of Germans; when other political parties were abolished and the Nazi party "was" Germany, opposition to it meant opposition to Germany. It seems that nothing is more difficult for the average man to bear than the feeling of not being identified with a larger group. However much a German citizen may be opposed to the principles of Nazism, if he has to choose between being alone and feeling that he belongs to Germany, most persons will choose the latter. It can be observed in many instances that persons who are not Nazis nevertheless defend Nazism against criticism of foreigners because they feel that an attack on Nazism is an attack on Germany. The fear of isolation and the relative weakness of moral principles help any party to win the loyalty of a large sector of the population once that party has captured the power of the state. . . .

In contrast to the negative or resigned attitude of the working class and of the liberal and Catholic bourgeoisie, the Nazi ideology was ardently greeted by the lower strata of the middle class, composed of small shopkeepers, artisans, and white-collar workers.

Members of the older generation among this class formed the more passive mass basis; their sons and daughters were the more active fighters. For them the Nazi ideology—its spirit of blind obedience to a leader and of hatred against racial and political minorities, its craving for conquest and domination, its exaltation of the German people and the "Nordic Race"—had a tremendous emotional appeal, and it was this appeal which won them over and made them into ardent believers in and fighters for the Nazi cause. The answer to the question why the Nazi ideology was so appealing to the lower middle class has to be sought for in the social character of the lower middle class. Their social character was markedly different from that of the working class, of the higher strata of the middle class, and of the nobility before the war of 1914. As a matter of fact, certain features were characteristic for this part of the middle class throughout its history: their love of the strong, hatred of the weak, their pettiness, hostility, thriftiness with feelings as well as with money, and essentially their asceticism. Their outlook on life was narrow, they suspected and hated the stranger, and they were curious and envious of their acquaintances, rationalizing their envy as moral indignation; their whole life was based on the principle of scarcity —economically as well as psychologically. . . .

The old middle class's feeling of powerlessness, anxiety, and isolation from the social whole and the destructiveness springing from this situation was not the only psychological source of Nazism. The peasants felt resentful against the urban creditors to whom they were in debt, while the workers felt deeply disappointed and discouraged by the constant political retreat after their first victories in 1918 under a leadership which had lost all strategic initiative. The vast majority of the population was seized with the feeling of individual insignificance and powerlessness which we have described as typical for monopolistic capitalism in general.

Those psychological conditions were not the "cause" of Nazism. They constituted its human basis without which it could not have developed, but any analysis of the whole phenomenon of the rise and victory of Nazism must deal with the strictly economic and political, as well as with the psychological, conditions. In view both of the literature dealing with this aspect and of the specific aims of this book, there is no need to enter into a discussion of these economic and political questions. The reader may be reminded, however, of the role which the representatives of big industry and the half-bankrupt Junkers played in the establishment of Nazism. Without their support Hitler could never have won, and their support was rooted in their understanding of their economic interests much more than in psychological factors. . . .

. . . The representatives of these privileged groups expected that Nazism would shift the emotional resentment which threatened them into other channels and at the same time harness the nation into the service of their own economic interests. On the whole they were not disappointed. To be sure, in minor details they were mistaken. Hitler and his bureaucracy were not tools to be ordered around by the Thyssens and Krupps, who had to share their power with the Nazi bureaucracy and often to submit to them. But although Nazism proved to be economically detrimental to all other classes, it fostered the interests of the most powerful groups of German industry. The Nazi system is the "streamlined" version of German prewar imperialism and it continued where the monarchy had failed. . . .

There is one question that many a reader will have in mind at this point: How can one reconcile the statement that the psychological basis of Nazism was the old middle class with the statement that Nazism functions in the interests of German imperialism? The answer to this question is in principle the same as that which was given to the question concerning the role of the urban middle class during the period of the rise of capitalism. In the postwar period it was the middle class, particularly the lower middle class, that was threatened by monopolistic capitalism. Its anxiety and thereby its hatred were aroused; it moved into a state of panic and was filled with a craving for submission to as well as for domination over those who were powerless. These feelings were used by an entirely different class for a regime which was to work for their own interests. Hitler proved to be such an efficient tool because he combined the characteristics of a resentful, hating, petty bourgeois, with whom the lower middle class could identify themselves emotionally and socially, with those of an opportunist who was ready to serve the interests of the German industrialists and Junkers. Originally he posed as the Messiah of the old middle class, promised the destruction of department stores, the breaking of the domination of banking capital, and so on. The record is clear enough. These promises were never fulfilled. However, that did not matter. Nazism never had any genuine political or economic principles. It is essential to understand that the very principle of Nazism is its radical opportunism. What mattered was that hundreds of thousands of petty bourgeois, who in the normal course of development had little chance to gain money or power, as members of the Nazi bureaucracy now got a large slice of the wealth and prestige they forced the upper classes to share with them. Others who were not members of the Nazi machine were given the jobs taken away from Jews and political enemies; and as for the rest, although they did not get more bread, they got "circuses." The emotional satisfaction afforded by these sadistic spectacles and by an ideology which gave them a feeling of superiority over the rest of mankind was able to compensate them—for a time at least—for the fact that their lives had been impoverished, economically and culturally.

. . . Hitler's personality, his teachings, and the Nazi system express an extreme form of the character structure which we have called "authoritarian" and . . . by this very fact he made a powerful appeal to those parts of the population which were—more or less—of the same character structure. . . .

. . . Hitler's writings [show] the two trends that we have already described as fundamental for the authoritarian character: the craving for power over men and the longing for submission to an overwhelmingly strong outside power. Hitler's ideas are more or less identical with the ideology of the Nazi party. The ideas expressed in his book are those which he expressed in the countless speeches by which he won mass following for his party. This ideology results from his personality which, with its inferiority feeling, hatred against life, asceticism, and envy of those who enjoy life, is the soil of sadomasochistic strivings; it was addressed to people who, on account of their similar character structure, felt attracted and excited by these teachings and became ardent followers of the man who expressed what they felt. But it was not only the Nazi ideology that satisfied the lower middle class; the political practice realized what the ideology promised. A hierarchy was created in which everyone has somebody above him to submit to and somebody beneath him to feel power over; the man at the top, the leader, has Fate, History, Nature above him as the power in which to submerge himself. Thus the Nazi ideology and practice satisfies the desires springing from the character structure of one part of the population and gives direction and orientation to those who, though not enjoying domination and submission, were resigned and had given up faith in life, in their own decisions, in everything.

Do these considerations give any clue for a prognosis with regard to the stability of Nazism in the future? I do not feel qualified to make any predictions. Yet a few points—such as those that follow from the psychological premises we have been discussing—would seem to be worth raising. Given the psychological conditions, does Nazism not fulfill the emotional needs of the population, and is this psychological function not one factor that makes for its growing stability?

From all that has been said so far, it is evident that the answer to this question is in the negative. The fact of human individuation, of the destruction of all "primary bonds," cannot be reversed. The process of the destruction of the medieval world has taken four hundred years and is being completed in our era. . . .

The function of an authoritarian ideology and practice can be compared to the function of neurotic symptoms. Such symptoms result from unbearable psychological conditions and at the same time offer a solution that makes life possible. Yet they are not a solution that leads to happiness or growth of personality. They leave unchanged the conditions that necessitate the neurotic solution. The dynamism of man's nature is an important factor that tends to seek for more satisfying solutions if there is a possibility of attaining them. The aloneness and powerlessness of the individual, his quest for the realization of potentialities which developed in him, the objective fact of the increasing productive capacity of modern industry, are dynamic factors, which constitute the basis for a growing quest for freedom and happiness. The escape into symbiosis can alleviate the suffering for a time but it does not eliminate it. The history of mankind is the history of growing individuation, but it is also the history of growing freedom. The quest for freedom is not a metaphysical force and cannot be explained by natural law; it is the necessary result of the process of individuation and of the growth of culture. The authoritarian systems cannot do away with the basic conditions that make for the quest for freedom; neither can they exterminate the quest for freedom that springs from these conditions.

Peter F. Drucker

FASCISM AS THE END OF ECONOMIC MAN

Peter F. Drucker (b. Vienna, 1909) was trained in German universities before coming to the United States in 1937. During a distinguished career as an educator and business consultant, he has been concerned with the social and political problems of industrial society. Since retiring as Professor of Business Management at New York University in 1962, he has continued to write and lecture on industrialism and the modern corporation.

Within a few short years fascist totalitarianism has assumed the proportions of a major world revolution. It has become the only effective political force in Europe, and has reduced democracy to impotent defence internally and externally. Fascist ideology and phraseology are accepted as a cloak by divergent and incongruous movements all over the world. The new nationalism in the Near East, the old feudalism of the Far East, traditional coup d'état's and "racial awakenings" in Latin America, religious revolts in the Asiatic or African colonial empires call themselves "totalitarian" in the same way in which such movements would have sailed thirty years ago under the democratic, and ten years ago under the communist, flag. And communism—the world revolution of yesterday—has not only been forced to admit that it has become purely defensive, but also that it has lost its fight. Whatever mental reservations the communist leaders might have made regarding the distant future, their drive for a united front with the bourgeoisie and with capitalist democracy against fascism amounts to complete abdication as a revolutionary force, and to virtual renunciation of the promise to be harbingers of the

From Peter F. Drucker, The End of Economic Man (London, 1939), pp. 3–22, 43–44, 47, 51–52, 56–58, 62–64, 74–75, 77–80. Copyright © 1939 by Peter F. Drucker. Reprinted by permission of John Cushman Associates, Inc., and Curtis Brown, Ltd.

future social order. The impotence of the "popular front" in France, and the complete collapse of the united front idea altogether over the Czechoslovak crisis, meant the end of communism as an effective resistance to fascism.

The rapid ascendancy of totalitarianism is all the more spectacular in view of the general hostility which it meets abroad. Everywhere there is nothing but horror of its brutality, fear of its aggressiveness, revulsion from its slogans and its gospel of hate. Unlike any earlier revolution, not even the minority in the countries of the old order accepts the tenets, the spirit, and the achievements of totalitarianism. And yet, fascism has been gaining ground steadily until it has become master of Europe.

Why has the solid opposition of the democracies been unable to check this greatest danger to all they believe in? It cannot have been cowardice. The heroism of the thousands who have laid down their lives in Spain for the sake of fighting fascism, of the Austrian workers who sacrificed themselves, or of the unsung, anonymous underground workers in Italy and Germany, is beyond doubt. If courage could have stopped totalitarianism it would have been stopped.

The reason why all resistance to the fascist menace has proved unavailing is that we do not know what we fight. We know the symptoms of fascism, but we do not know its causes and its meaning. And the very people who have made resistance to fascism the main article of their creed by calling themselves antifascists insist upon fighting a phantom of their own invention. This ignorance is the main cause, both of the complacent hope of one section of public opinion in the democratic countries that the "radicalism" of fascism is but a passing phase and of the antifascist illusion that fascism "cannot last," which together have been responsible for the ineffectiveness of democratic resistance. The analysis of the causes of fascism would therefore appear to be our most important task.

The attempt to understand rationally the phenomenon of fascism is not, as is frequently asserted by people whose emotion gets the better of their judgment, a defence of and apology for fascism, but on the contrary the only basis from which a successful fight against its world-wide spread can be waged.

As a revolution which threatens every concept on which European civilization has been based, fascism has its roots in European developments. To what extent the same forces which produced fascism in Europe are effective and active in the United States as well, I am not qualified to determine. But I firmly believe that this country is so dissimilar and contains such strong independent forces of its own as to make invalid any direct application of my conclusions to American conditions. I hope that this analysis of the causes and of the meaning of fascism will serve a real purpose in this country; but not that of inducing my American readers to apply European clichés to their own country.

Apart from the assertion that the majority of the people in the fascist countries are secretly hostile to the regime and are only held down by terror, which is such a flagrant perversion of all evidence as to require no specific refutation, three explanations of the nature of fascism are generally offered: (1) fascism is a malicious outbreak of primitive barbarity and brutality; or (2) it is a temporarily successful attempt of the capitalists to delay or to prevent the final, inevitable victory of socialism; or (3) it is the result of the impact of unscrupulous and technically perfect propaganda upon the gullible masses and their basest instincts.

Every one of these assertions is meaningless as an explanation of the nature and the causes of totalitarianism. It is certainly true that fascism excels in sanguinary brutality and wanton cruelty, and that it tramples on life and liberty of the individual. In the eyes of the writer, who believes in an absolute good and evil, this alone would be sufficient reason to condemn fascism in its entirety. But it does not explain anything. Brutality and cruelty are in themselves only symptoms that fascism is a revolution which, like all revolutions, shakes men out of their customary routine tracks and releases their hidden ferocious instincts. Brutality, cruelty, and bloodshed are characteristics of every revolution, regardless of its causes, nature, and direction. The forces of destruction are as evil as they are blind.

As for the explanation that fascism is a last desperate attempt of capitalism to delay the socialist revolution, it simply is not true. It is not true that "big business" promoted fascism. On the contrary, both in Italy and in Germany the proportion of fascist sympathizers and backers was smallest in the industrial and banking classes. It is equally untrue that "big business" profits from fascism; of all the classes it probably suffers most from totalitarian economics and *Wehrwirtschaft*. And finally, it is just ridiculous to maintain that the capitalist class—or, for that matter, anybody else—had reason to fear a victory of the working classes in prefascist Italy and Germany. The whole thesis is nothing but a feeble attempt to reconcile Marxist theory with the facts by falsifying history; it is a lame apology but not a serious explanation.

The most dangerous and at the same time most stupid explanation of fascism is the propaganda theory. In the first place, I have never been able to find anyone who could reconcile it with the fact that right up to the fascist victory—and in Italy beyond it—literally all means of propaganda were in the hands of uncompromising enemies of fascism. There was not one widely-read newspaper but poured ridicule on Hitler

and Mussolini while the Nazi and the fascist press were unread and on
the verge of bankruptcy. The radio in Germany, owned by the government, issued one anti-Nazi broadside after the other. More powerful than
both, the established churches used all the enormous direct influence of
the pulpit and of the confessional to fight fascism and Nazism.

But this is a minor matter compared to the shortsightedness which
can deceive itself into using as an argument *against* fascism that the
masses have been doped by propaganda. For this would be an argument
only in support of fascism; and Hitler has indeed used it as such in his
Mein Kampf. In fighting against fascism we profess to fight for democracy and freedom, for individual liberty and for the inalienable rights
and dignity of man. If we ourselves admit that the masses can be lured
by propaganda to give up these rights, there can be no justification at
all for our creed and we had better become fascists ourselves. This
would at least be more sincere and less harmful than the pretentiousness
of the fake aristocratism which, while bemoaning the decline of freedom
and liberty, fears the "revolt of the masses."

But to deny liberty and self-determination to the masses in order to
shield them from propaganda is no alternative to fascism; nor would
absence of propaganda have prevented its spread. Learned scholars in
learned books on mass psychology have come to the conclusion that it
is owing only to the chance absence of the right type of demagogic
mass-leader that we do not go on all fours or are not all nudists, since
the masses "probably" fall easy prey to any superior salesman, whatever
his goods. Yet it is as true today as it ever was that propaganda only
converts those who already believe, and only appeals to people if it
answers an existing need or allays an existing fear. The success of a certain type of propaganda and its reasons are valuable symptoms. But
propaganda is not a cause, nor is counterpropaganda a cure.

That the antifascist movements content themselves with these attempts at explanation—partly untrue, partly meaningless, always superficial—is not just an accident. It is the logical result of their fundamental self-deception and delusion. They refuse to see and to realize
that the "total state" of fascism is not a political alignment *within* the
existing political and social setup, but that it is a revolution which, like
all revolutions, works from *without.* To the antifascist the world is still
unchanged in its essentials and fascism must fit in somehow. Actually,
fascism has already changed or destroyed those essentials of yesterday,
as is shown by the fact that every nation would have to go totalitarian
in the event of war. For, as long as war remains a means of politics, any
radical change in the social organization of warfare such as has been
wrought by "total war" with its new weapons and its new concept of

belligerents, indicates a profound revolutionary change in the social and political order.

The illusion that a revolution is not a revolution, but one of the old forces in a new disguise, has always been entertained by the ancien régime. That only a small minority supports the new movement and that, moreover, its victories are entirely due to rabble-rousing and to the stirring-up of the basest instincts, was held as stubbornly by the Popes in the sixteenth century as by the Cavaliers in the seventeenth and by the French aristocracy in the eighteenth. This illusion has always been the main reason why the forces of the old order were defeated. A revolution can only be overcome if it is recognized as such and if its true causes are diagnosed correctly. And the true cause, the only possible cause, of a revolution is a fundamental and radical change in the order of values, especially in that most important sphere, man's conception of his own nature and of his place in the universe and in society.

If we want to understand what distinguishes fascism from the revolutions of the past, we have to start with the symptoms which are new and particular to it. Therefore we can disregard its terror, its ruthless persecution of dissenters and minorities, and its cruelty and brutality as typical of revolutions in general. The same holds true of the outward form of military dictatorship and even of the fact that the dictator came from below and did not belong to the "polite society" of the old order. Finally, contrary to general opinion, the combination of "formal legality" and open illegality of the revolutionary movement has been common in some degree to all European revolutions ever since centralized government replaced feudal decentralization long before Cromwell.

The novel and therefore differentiating symptoms are threefold:

1. Fascist totalitarianism has no positive ideology, but confines itself to refuting, fighting, and denying all traditional ideas and ideologies.

2. Fascism not only refutes all old ideas but denies, for the first time in European history, the foundation on which all former political and social systems had been built: the justification of the social and political system and of the authority constituted under it as the only means to further the true well-being of the individual subjected to it.

3. The masses joined fascism not because they believe in its promises, which take the place of a positive creed, but *because they do not believe in them.*

We have the testimony of Mussolini himself, who repeatedly boasted

that fascism, when it came to power, had no positive policy, no programme, and no system. Only afterwards were the historians and philosophers commissioned to fashion an ideology. Hitler is less frank and
probably also less clear-headed; but the positive creed of Nazism: the
worship of the old Germanic gods, the Nordic perfect man, the corporate state composed of self-governing, autonomous "estates," and the
heroic family, has remained in the books. The masses are not interested
in these concepts and ideas; not even the best-organized mass meeting
shows any enthusiasm for them. And it was certainly not these mystical
new articles of faith which brought frenzied mass support to Hitler.

Mussolini—and Hitler, imitating him—have tried to make an asset
out of the lack of a positive creed and a system out of having none. That,
and nothing else, is the meaning of Mussolini's "men make history"!
In so far as this was meant to read, "Mussolini makes history," the slogan
is neither particularly original nor in any way important. But Mussolini
meant much more: he wanted to claim that the deed is before the
thought, and that revolution logically precedes the development of a
new creed or of a new economic order. Historically, this is nonsense.
All revolutions of the past have been caused by protracted and profound
developments either in the intellectual sphere or in the social, or in both.
The "great historical figure" at best provided the ignition and was
often only a tool. Mussolini's contention is, however, correct—or partly
correct—insofar as it applies to the fascist and Nazi revolutions. There
the "deed"—i.e., the revolution—took place without the previous development of a positive creed or of a new socioeconomic order.

But if there is no positive creed in totalitarianism, there is as com-
pensation an abundance of negatives. Of course, every revolution repudi-
ates what went on before and considers itself a conscious break with the
past; it is only posterity that sees, or imagines it sees, the historical continuity. Fascism, however, goes much further in its negation of the past
than any earlier political movement, because it makes this negation its
main platform. What is even more important, it denies simultaneously
ideas and tendencies which are in themselves antithetic. It is antiliberal,
but also anticonservative; antireligious and antiatheist; anticapitalist and
antisocialist; antiwar and antipacifist; against big business, but also
against the small artisans and shopkeepers who are regarded as superfluous—the list could be continued indefinitely. It is typical that the
leitmotiv of all Nazi propaganda is not the "Nordic man," not the
promises, conquests, and achievements of Nazism, but *anti-Semitism*,
the attack against the "fourteen years" before Hitler and against foreign
conspiracy. The Nazi agitator whom, many years ago, I heard proclaim
to a wildly cheering peasants' meeting: *"We don't want lower bread*

prices, we don't want higher bread prices, we don't want unchanged bread prices—we want National-Socialist bread prices," came nearer explaining fascism than anybody I have heard since. But for the sentimental invocation of the glory of the Rome of the Caesars, which is anyhow too far away to be a living tradition, Italian fascism works in the same way.

Of these denials of European tradition one is especially important: that is the refutation of the demand that the political and social order and the authority set up under it have to justify themselves as benefiting their subjects. Hardly any other concept or idea of our past is held up to so much ridicule by fascism as that of the justification of power. "Power is its own justification" is regarded as self-evident. Nothing shows better how far the totalitarian revolution has already gone than the general acceptance of this new maxim throughout Europe as a matter of course. Actually it is the most startling innovation. For the last two thousand years, ever since Aristotle, the justification of power and authority has been the central problem of European political thought and of European political history. And since Europe became Christian there has never been any other approach to this problem than that of seeking justification in the benefit which the exercise of power confers upon its subjects—be it the salvation of their souls, the "good life," or the highest standard of living for the greatest number. Not even the most fanatical advocate of absolute monarchy would have dared to justify the sovereign otherwise. The German Protestant clerics of the sixteenth century who developed the idea of the divine right of autocracy, as well as Hobbes and Bossuet, took the greatest pains to prove the benefits for the subjects. The infinite contempt in which Machiavelli has been held by contemporaries and posterity is entirely due to his indifference to the moral justification of authority, which made this conscientious and honest man appear a moral leper even in the corrupt and power-obsessed world of the Italian Renaissance. In every social system that bases itself on the European tradition, the justification of power must be the central problem. For it is through this concept alone that freedom and equality—or, as was formerly said, justice—can be projected into the social and political reality; and freedom and equality have been Europe's basic spiritual ideas ever since the introduction of Christianity. But to fascism the problem does not even exist except as a ridiculous relic of "Jewish liberalism."

Even more important as a symptom of the true nature of fascism is the psychology of its appeal to the masses. The emphasis laid upon the "propaganda" explanation by practically all students of the problem—fascist and others—implicitly recognizes its importance. The maxim that "a lie becomes accepted as the truth if it is only repeated often enough" would seem to be an obvious and easily understandable explanation; but it happens to be the wrong one. Nothing impressed me more in Germany in the years before Hitler than the almost universal disbelief in the Nazi promises and the indifference toward the Nazi creed among the most fanatical Nazis. Outside the party ranks this disbelief turned into open ridicule. And yet the masses flocked to the Nazi fold.

One example—the case of the Boxheim Documents—shows to the full the inner contradiction of the belief in Nazi propaganda. Some time before Hitler came to power a memorandum in which a group of young Nazis had tried to formulate their picture of the coming Nazi state became public through an indiscretion. They had followed closely the official party programme, Hitler's speeches, and his book. The result was a forecast that has proved astonishingly correct. Yet, although no other conclusion could have been reached on the basis of the Nazi tenets, the publication of the document provoked boundless laughter—in the Nazi ranks. I talked at the time with a great number of convinced Nazis—students, small shopkeepers, white-collar workers, and unemployed—and there was not one but was sincerely convinced that the thing was an absurdity and that only the most stupid and most ignorant person could really believe that the Nazi creed and the Nazi tenets could or would be realized. "Life under such conditions would be impossible and unbearable" was the unanimous and sincere conclusion of all these devoted Nazis, every one of whom was ready to die for the party.

Equally striking is the fact that racial anti-Semitism was not taken seriously even by the great majority of Nazis. "It is just a catchword to attract voters" was a standing phrase which everybody repeated and believed, and that I took it seriously was more than once regarded as definite proof of my stupidity and guillibility.

The same contradiction appeared in the vital issue of war or peace. That the German people feared war as much as any other nation in Europe was undoubtedly true before 1933, and it is hardly less true today. It was obvious to everyone that Hitler's foreign policy must mean war in the long run. Yet every Nazi believed and still believes Hitler's protestations of his peaceful intentions.

The masses must have known that Hitler's promises were incompatible each with the other. They may have been taken in in spiritual matters such as the simultaneity of rabid anti-Christian propaganda with equally fervent assertions that Nazism is the savior of the churches. But German farmers trained by a hundred years of cooperative organization, and German workers after sixty years of trade-unionism and collective bargaining, could not have failed to notice the glaring conflict between simultaneous promises—such as, for instance, those made by Dr. Goebbels in one and the same speech in 1932—that the farmer would receive more for his grain, the worker pay less for his bread, and the baker and grocer have a higher wholesale and retail margin. And what about the Berlin metalworkers' strike in 1932—one of the most embittered labour conflicts in German history—when the Nazis together with the Communists supported the strike against the official trade unions who had called it off, while Hitler at the very same moment promised the extremely class-conscious metal manufacturers in a public speech that under Nazism they would again be master in their own house? Result: half the workers and almost all the industrialists turned Nazi. Yet no propaganda could have made employers in the Berlin metal industry or German workers overlook or forget such a contradiction. Or what about Hitler's oath in court that his movement relied entirely on "legal means," while at the same time he made some Nazis "honorary members of the Party" in an enthusiastic telegram reprinted everywhere, as a reward for having murdered an unarmed and defenceless opponent?

Nor should it be forgotten that these astonishing feats were witnessed by a hostile press, a hostile radio, a hostile cinema, a hostile church, and a hostile government which untiringly pointed out the Nazi lies, the Nazi inconsistency, the unattainability of their promises, and the dangers and folly of their course. Clearly, nobody would have been a Nazi if rational belief in the Nazi promises had been a prerequisite.

In addition, the Nazi leaders themselves never pretended to speak the truth. Beginning with Hitler's frank admission in his book that lying is necessary, Nazi leaders have prided themselves publicly on their disregard for truth and on the impossibility of their promises—foremost among them Dr. Goebbels. Not once but several times have I heard him say in mass meetings when the people cheered a particularly choice lie: "Of course, you understand all this is just propaganda"; and the masses only cheered louder.

The same thing happened in Austria; the same thing in Czechoslovakia; the same thing, I understand, with slight modifications, in prefascist Italy. Is there any other explanation than that the masses believed in fascism although—or perhaps even because—they did not believe its promises?

These three main characteristics peculiar to fascism: the absence of a positive creed and the overemphasis on the refutation of the whole past, the denial of the demand for the justification of power, and the trust of the masses in fascism in spite of their lack of belief in its statements and promises, are the symptoms on which any serious diagnosis has to be based. They are in themselves symptoms only, though important ones, and they do not explain fascism. But they show where the disease is located, and they indicate the order and species to which it belongs.

Of the three, the first is easiest to understand and to place. The overemphasis on the negative is clearly meant to offset the absence of a positive creed. It shows that, in spite of Mussolini and Hitler, deeds do not come before thought, but that a revolution has to have a creed; if a genuinely positive new creed is unavailable, the negative must be substituted. This means that the fascist revolution, like all European revolutions, has its roots in developments in the spiritual, intellectual, and social field and not, as the fascists themselves pretend, in that of action. There is only one fundamental difference to the usual—but not, as will be shown later, the invariable—pattern. In the typical revolution the old orders, systems, and creeds break down simultaneously with the emergence of a new order. The fascist revolution, like all its predecessors, has been caused by the breakdown of the old order from within. But in marked contrast to historical precedent no new positive creed appeared as soon as the old one collapsed.

This supplies also the explanation for the fascist attitude toward the justification of power which has been the mainstay of all orders and creeds of the European past. There can be no doubt that fascism, which suffers so acutely from the lack of a positive creed, would have availed itself of a solution continuing the European tradition, had one existed. The break with freedom and equality and with the justification of power implies, therefore, that there is, at least at present, no way to continue the European tradition and to derive a new solution from it. Inability to develop the European basic concepts any further in the direction in which they had been moving the last few hundred years must obviously be the fundamental cause of fascism.

This assumption is supported by our third symptom: the psychology of the attraction of fascism, which also elucidates the nature of its new solution. At first sight this psychology might appear as something most extraordinary and complicated. But in ordinary life we meet it all the time, and we know without difficulty what it means if somebody believes against belief. The small boy who has smashed the jar while stealing the jam knows that he will be discovered and punished; but he prays, hopes, and believes against belief that he will escape. During the last few years the British Government has been doing the same thing. It knows that there is no lasting peace with the dictators; but it believes against belief, hopes against hope, that it can be found. Both the boy and the British Government hope for a miracle. The boy hopes for the intervention of his guardian angel or for a nice fire that would cover up his tracks by burning the house. The British Government, since it is composed of mature men, asks fate for much more unlikely miracles: it hopes for a revolution in Germany, an economic smash-up, or a Russo-German war. Both make themselves believe in a miracle against all reason and knowledge because the alternative is too terrible to face. Both turn to the miracle because they are in despair. And so are the masses when they turn to fascism.

The old orders have broken down, and no new order can be contrived from the old foundations. The alternative is chaos; and in despair the masses turn to the magician who promises to make the impossible possible: to make the workers free and simultaneously to make the industrialist "master in his own house"; to increase the price of wheat and at the same time to lower the price of bread; to bring peace, yet to bring victory in war; to be everything to everybody and all things to all men. So it is not in spite of but because of its contradictions and its impossibility that the masses turn to fascism. For if you are caught between the flood of a past, through which you cannot retrace your steps, and an apparently unscalable blank wall in front of you, it is only by magic and miracles that you can hope to escape. *Credo quia absurdum*, that cry of a master who had known all the bitterness of deepest and blackest despair, is heard again for the first time in many a century.

The despair of the masses is the key to the understanding of fascism. No "revolt of the mob," no "triumphs of unscrupulous propaganda," but stark despair caused by the breakdown of the old order and the absence of a new one.

What broke down? Why and how? What miracle has fascism to fulfill? How does it try and can it do it? Will there be a new order? When and on what basis? These questions I have to answer in the following analysis. I will anticipate only one point: the abracadabra of fascism is the substitution of *organization* for creed and order; though it cannot succeed and cannot last, the formal democracy of capitalism and of socialism cannot prevent its spread. But the glorification of organization as an end in itself shows that eventually there will be a new order based upon a reformulation of the old fundamental values of European tradition: freedom and equality. . . .

II

Every organized society is built upon a concept of the nature of man and of his function and place in society. Whatever its truth as a picture of human nature, this concept always gives a true picture of the nature of the society which recognizes and identifies itself with it. It symbolizes the fundamental tenets and beliefs of society by showing the sphere of human activity which it regards as socially decisive and supreme. The concept of man as an "economic animal" is the true symbol of the societies of bourgeois capitalism and of Marxist socialism, which see in the free exercise of man's economic activity the means toward the realization of their aims. Economic satisfactions alone appear socially important and relevant. Economic positions, economic privileges, and economic rights are those for which man works. For these he wages war, and for these he is prepared to die. All others seem mere hypocrisy, snobbism, or romantic nonsense.

This concept of Economic Man found its first literary expression in the *homo œconomicus* of Adam Smith and his school. He was their all-cunning and completely unscrupulous fictional character, who not only always wanted to act according to his best economic interests, but also always knew how to do so. This abstraction, though useful in a textbook, was, of course, too crude and too much of a caricature to be accepted as a real definition of man's true nature. Even bourgeois capitalism adopted Marx's refined and corrected edition of the Economic Man who, in the last analysis, will tend to act according to his "class interests," even if he neither wants to do it nor knows that he does it. . . .

The collapse of the society of Economic Man was inevitable as soon as Marxism had proved itself unable to realize the free and equal society. Beyond Marxism there is no possibility of reconciling the supremacy of the economic sphere with the belief in freedom and equality as the true aims of society. And the only justification, the only basis for Economic Man or for any society based thereon, is the promise of the realization of freedom and equality. . . .

With the collapse of Marxism as a creed, any society based upon the sovereignty and autonomy of the economic sphere becomes invalid and irrational, because freedom and equality cannot be realized in it and through it. But while the old orders of capitalism and socialism disintegrated beyond revival and beyond possibility of further development, no new order arose. As we have seen above, it is the characteristic feature of our times that no new concept of the nature of man lies ready under the surface to take the place of Economic Man. No new sphere of human activity offers itself for the projection of freedom and equality. While Europe becomes, therefore, unable to explain and to justify its old social orders with and from its old concepts, it has not as yet acquired or developed a new concept from which new valid social values, a new reason for a new order, and an explanation of man's place in it could be derived.

Through the collapse of Economic Man the individual is deprived of his social order, and his world of its rational existence. He can no longer explain or understand his existence as rationally correlated and coordinated to the world in which he lives; nor can he coordinate the world and the social reality to his existence. The function of the individual in society has become entirely irrational and senseless. Man is isolated within a tremendous machine, the purpose and meaning of which he does not accept and cannot translate into terms of his experience. Society ceases to be a community of individuals bound together by a common purpose, and becomes a chaotic hubbub of purposeless isolated monads.

This disintegration of the rational character of society and of the rational relationship between individual and society is the most revolutionary trait of our times. . . .

III

The collapse of the belief in the capitalist and socialist creeds was translated into terms of individual experience by the [First] World War and the Great Depression. These catastrophes broke through the everyday routine which makes men accept existing forms, institutions, and tenets as unalterable natural laws. They suddenly exposed the vacuum behind the façade of society. The European masses realized for the first time that existence in this society is governed not by rational and sensible, but by blind, irrational, and demonic forces.

Modern war appeared to be the denial of all tenets on which the mechanical and rational conception of society is based. This was not because war is amechanical and arational, but because it reduces mechanization and rationalization to absurdity. The machine and the rational, strategical, or economic calculation to which men are just so many impersonal units become autonomous forces of their own. They appear as entirely independent of the control or understanding of the subjugated individual, and therefore as entirely irrational. In terms of human experience the war showed the individual suddenly as an isolated, helpless, powerless atom in a world of irrational monsters. The concept of society in which man is an equal and free member and in which his

fate depends mainly upon his own merits and his own efforts, proved
an illusion. . . .

The Great Depression proved that irrational and incalculable forces
also rule peacetime society: the threats of sudden permanent unemployment, of being thrown on the industrial scrap heap in one's prime or
even before one has started to work. Against these forces the individual
finds himself as helpless, isolated, and atomized as against the forces of
machine war. He cannot determine when unemployment is going to hit
and why; he cannot fight it, he cannot even dodge it. Like the forces of
war, the forces of depression reduce man's rational and mechanical concept of his own existence to absurdity, because they are the ultimate
consequences of his rational and mechanical society. And like the forces
of war, depression shows man as a senseless cog in a senselessly whirling
machine which is beyond human understanding and which has ceased
to serve any purpose but its own.

These experiences are not due to anything inherent in the character of
war and depression as such. They are exclusively due to the disintegration
of the belief in the foundations of our society. It becomes impossible to
coordinate the rational existence of the individual to a society which
breeds wars and depressions. As far as modern war is concerned, it will,
of course, always be regarded as a terrible evil. But that it appears irrational and senseless is not a necessary consequence. To both sides in the
civil war in Spain modern warfare appears rational in spite of its terror.
The [First] World War came to appear senseless and chaotic only because it revealed the main foundation of the social order as illusory.
Otherwise the war would have made sense as part of this rational order.
The sacrifices of the individual would have appeared as a major tribute
to the order and as the highest confirmation of its fundamental truth,
in the same spirit in which they were regarded by the soldiers of the
French Revolution or by the Prussian and Austrian volunteers who rose
against Napoleon in 1813. . . .

For the common man it is completely irrelevant whether the irrationality of war and depression is owing to changes in their character or
to changes in his own beliefs. The individual does not care whether the
forces which govern society have become irrational or whether it is the
breakdown of his own rational concept of society which deprives them
of their rational explanation and their rational function. The fact that
the world has no order and follows no laws is all that is important to

him. For the last hundred years economists have unsuccessfully tried to discover the causes of the business cycle. The best of them always knew that they could not do much more than understand the last depression. And that there are only losers in war has been a commonplace for time untold. But the individual is not concerned with historical "proofs," demonstrating that the world has not changed. All he need understand is that the attempt to comprise the universe in a mechanically rational order, in which life and death could be understood in terms of a calculable, logical sequence, has resulted in the *return of the demons* as the real masters of his destiny.

These new demons—poison gas and bombs from the air, permanent unemployment, and "too old at forty"—are all the more terrible because they are man-made. The demons of old were as natural as their manifestations in earthquakes or storms. The new demons, though no less inescapable, are unnatural. They can be released by man only; but once they have been turned loose, man has no control over them—less than he had over the tribal gods of the ancients or over the djinns of the *Arabian Nights*, who could always be placated by magic, prayer, or sacrifice. The new demons are far more unbearable than the old ones ever were. A Kierkegaard, a Dostoevski, an isolated, consciously lonely poet or philosopher, might be able to look at them unflinchingly and yet remain sane. The average individual cannot bear the utter atomization, the unreality and senselessness, the destruction of all order, of all society, of all rational individual existence through blind, incalculable, senseless forces created as result of rationalization and mechanization.

To banish these new demons has become the paramount objective of European society. . . .

The masses, then, have become prepared to abandon freedom if this promises to reestablish the rationality of the world. If freedom is incompatible with equality, they will give up freedom. If it is incompatible with security, they will decide for security. To be free or not has become a secondary question, since the freedom available does not help to banish the demons. Since the "free" society is the one which is threatened by the demons, it seems more than plausible to blame freedom and to expect delivery from despair through the abandonment of freedom.

The form in which Europe has cast away freedom is, however, very peculiar. Not even in Nazi Germany has freedom been denounced as an abstract concept. On the contrary, the less real freedom there is, the more there is talk of the "new freedom." Yet this new freedom is a mere word which covers the exact contradiction of all that Europe ever understood by freedom. . . .

This is a most important and unprecedented characteristic of our time. The mere façade of slogans and forms is being maintained as an empty shell while the whole structure has to be abandoned. The more intolerable the substance of the industrial order becomes for the masses, the more necessary does it become to retain its outward forms.

In this contradiction is the true cause of fascism. It springs from the basic experience of the epoch in which we live: the absence of a new creed and of a new order. The old order has ceased to have validity and reality, and its world has therefore become irrational and demonic. But there has emerged no new order which would have brought a new basis of belief, and from which we could develop new forms and new institutions to organize social reality so as to enable us to attain a new supreme goal. We cannot maintain the substance of our old order, since it brings spiritual chaos, which the masses cannot bear. But neither can we abandon the old forms and institutions, as this would bring social and economic chaos, which is equally unbearable. To find a way out which gives a new substance, which carries a new rationality, and which makes possible at the same time the maintenance of the old outward forms is the demand of the masses in their despair. And it is this task which fascism sets out to accomplish.

The very nature of this task explains the stress laid upon "legality" and "legal continuity" which has been puzzling so many observers and which has been responsible for the failure to recognize the revolutionary character of the movement. According to all historical experience, a revolution glories in breaking the old façades and in producing new forms, new institutions, and new slogans. But—as discerning observers noticed while the revolution was still in progress—the social substance changes only slowly and often not at all. In fascism the substance of the old order has been ruthlessly destroyed. But the most superficial old form is carefully preserved. No previous revolution would have retained Hindenburg as president of the German Republic while abolishing the republic of which he was the president. This perversion of all historical rule is inevitable in fascism, which has to maintain the forms while destroying the substance.

That fascism opposes and abolishes all freedom, stems by equal necessity from its assignment. Since it is caused by the absence of a new sphere of human activity into which freedom could be projected, the new substance which it attempts to give to society must by necessity be an unfree substance of an unfree society. By equal necessity all freedom must appear hostile to the unfree new goal, the attainment of which depends upon complete compulsion and complete submission. Therefore fascism by its nature must deny all tenets, all concepts, all articles of the faith of Europe, because all of them were built on the concept of freedom. Its own creed must become all the more negative as it becomes the more difficult to save the forms, catchwords, and ornaments of the empty façade of Europe's past.

Finally, the nature of fascism explains why it has to turn against reason and why it is believed against belief. It can accomplish its task through a miracle only. To maintain the very outward forms which provoke the demons and to give a new substance which banishes or rationalizes the same demons, is a contradiction which reason cannot resolve. But it must be solved because the masses can bear the despair of complete senselessness as little as they can bear that of social chaos. They must turn their hopes toward a miracle. In the depths of their despair reason cannot be believed, truth must be false, and lies must be truth. "Higher bread prices," "lower bread prices," "unchanged bread prices" have all failed. The only hope lies in a kind of bread price which is none of these, which nobody has ever seen before, and which belies the evidence of one's reason.

It is not in spite of its being contrary to reason and in spite of its rejecting everything of the past without exception, but because of it, that the masses flocked to fascism and Nazism and that they abandoned themselves to Mussolini and Hitler. The sorcerer is a sorcerer because he does supernatural things in a supernatural way unknown to all reasonable tradition and contrary to all laws of logic. And it is a sorcerer able to work powerful miracles that the masses in Europe demand and need to allay their intolerable terror of a world which the demons have reconquered.

FASCISM AS TOTALITARIANISM

Carl J. Friedrich and Zbigniew K. Brzezinski

FASCISM AS TOTALITARIANISM: MEN AND TECHNOLOGY

Carl J. Friedrich (b. Leipzig, 1901) was educated in Germany before coming to the United States in 1922. During a long and honored career as Professor of Government at Harvard University, he served as advisor to various national and international agencies, and to political leaders in Europe and America. He was one of the earliest and most original thinkers on the subject of totalitarian government.

Zbigniew K. Brzezinski (b. Warsaw, 1928) was educated in Canada and the United States and has taught political science and government at Harvard and Columbia University. He is a recognized authority on Soviet affairs and has held high advisory posts in the American government on questions involving the Communist bloc.

The present study of totalitarian dictatorship seeks to give a general, descriptive theory of a novel form of government. It does not seek to explain why this dictatorship came into being, for the authors are convinced that such an explanation is not feasible at the present time, though some of the essential conditions can be described. . . .

THE GENERAL CHARACTERISTICS OF TOTALITARIAN DICTATORSHIP

Everybody talks about totalitarian dictatorships and about totalitarianism. They are said to be tyrannies, despotisms, absolutisms. And yet, the

From Carl J. Friedrich and Zbigniew K. Brzezinski, Totalitarian Dictatorship and Autocracy (Cambridge, Mass.: Harvard University Press, 1956), pp. vii, 3, 5–13, 17–20, 24–27, 29, 38–39, 80–81, 84–85, 87–89, 293–95, 297–303. Copyright 1956 by the President and Fellows of Harvard College. By permission of the authors and Harvard University Press. A second edition of this work, revised by Professor Friedrich in the light of new developments and research, was published in 1965.

greatest uncertainty surrounds the most elementary aspects of this form of government. One flatters it, actually, when one calls a dictatorship of this kind a tyranny or a despotism. The autocratic regimes of the past were not nearly as ghastly as the totalitarian dictatorships of our time. Yet, one also maligns totalitarian dictatorship by these descriptions, for, whereas tyranny was conducted, according to the definition of Aristotle, for the benefit of the tyrant, it is not very realistic to make that kind of egoism the basis of an interpretation of totalitarian dictatorship.

The truth of the matter seems to be that totalitarian dictatorship is a logical extension of certain traits of our modern industrial society (oftentimes called "capitalism"). . . . It is our contention . . . that totalitarian dictatorship is historically unique and *sui generis*. It is also our conclusion from all the facts available to us that fascist and communist totalitarian dictatorships are basically alike, or at any rate more nearly like each other than like any other system of government, including earlier forms of autocracy. These two theses are closely linked and must be examined together. They are also linked to a third, that totalitarian dictatorship as it actually developed was not intended by those who created it—Mussolini talked of it, but meant something different —but resulted from the political situations in which the anticonstitutionalist and antidemocratic revolutionary movements and their leaders found themselves. Let us take the third of these points first, treating the second and first afterward.

The fascist and communist systems evolved in response to a series of unprecedented crises, and they have shown a continuous, though intermittent, tendency to become more "totalitarian." There is no present reason to conclude that the existing totalitarian systems will disappear as a result of internal evolution, though this possibility cannot be excluded. The two totalitarian governments which have perished thus far have perished as the result of wars in which they had become involved with outside powers, but this does not mean that the Soviet Union necessarily will. We do not presuppose that totalitarian societies are fixed and static entities, but, on the contrary, that they have undergone and continue to undergo a steady evolution, presumably involving both growth and deterioration.

In terms of historical perspective, three points might be added. First, certain autocracies in the past have shown extraordinary capacity for survival. Not only the Roman but also several Oriental empires lasted for hundreds of years, at least as systems they did, though the dynasties changed. By contrast, the tyrannies of the Greek city-states were usually short-lived, as Aristotle noted. Second, such autocracies have as a rule perished in consequence of foreign invasions. Third, their autocratic features have usually been intensified over long periods, the reason being that violence is readily available for dealing with the tensions and break-downs that occur. In short, some of these autocracies were not stable, but lasting.

To the uncertainties about the end correspond the controversies about the beginning of totalitarian dictatorship. The debate about the causes or origins of totalitarianism has run all the way from a primitive bad-man theory to the "moral crisis of our time" kind of argument. A detailed inspection of the available evidence suggests that virtually every one of the factors which has been offered by itself as an explanation of the origin of totalitarian dictatorship has played its role. For example, in the case of Germany—Hitler's moral and personal defects, weaknesses in the German constitutional tradition, certain traits involved in the Ger-man "national character," the Versailles Treaty and its aftermath, the economic crisis and the "contradictions" of an aging capitalism, the "threat" of communism, the decline of Christianity and of such other spiritual moorings as the belief in the reason and the reasonableness of man—all have played a role in the total configuration of factors con-tributing to the overall result. As in the case of other broad develop-ments in history, only a multiple-factor analysis will do. But at the pres-ent time, we cannot fully explain the rise of totalitarian dictatorship. All we can do is to explain it partially by identifying some of the ante-cedent and concomitant conditions. Broadly speaking, totalitarian dic-tatorship is a new development; there has never been anything quite like it before.

Now concerning the second point, it is very important to explain somewhat at the outset why the totalitarian dictatorships, communist and fascist, are *basically alike*. What does this mean? In the first place, it means that they are *not wholly alike*. Popular and journalistic inter-pretation has oscillated between two extremes; some have said that the communist and fascist dictatorships are wholly alike, others that they are not at all alike. The latter view was the prevailing one during the popular-front days in Europe as well as in "liberal" circles in the United States. It was even more popular during the Second World War, espe-cially among Allied propagandists. Besides, it was and is the official Soviet and Hitler party line. It is only natural that these regimes, con-ceiving of themselves as bitter enemies, dedicated to the task of liqui-dating each other, should take the view that they have nothing in com-mon. This has happened before in history. When the Protestants and Catholics were fighting each other during the religious wars of the sixteenth and seventeenth centuries, they very commonly denied to each other the name of "Christians," and argued about each other that they were not "true churches." Actually, and from the viewpoint of the sectarians whom they both persecuted, they were indeed that.

The other view, that communist and fascist dictatorships are wholly alike, is presently favored in the United States and in Western Europe to an increasing extent. Yet they are obviously not wholly alike. For example, they differ in their proclaimed purposes and intentions. Everyone knows that the communists say they seek the world revolution of the proletariat, while the fascists proclaimed their determination to establish the world dominance of a particular nation or people, or at least their imperial predominance in a region, as in the case of the Italian Fascists. The communist and fascist dictatorships differ also in their historical antecedents: the fascist movements have arisen in reaction to the communist challenge and have offered themselves to a frightened middle class as the saviors from the communist danger. As we shall have occasion to show in the chapters which follow, there are many other differences which do not allow us to speak of the communist and fascist totalitarian dictatorships as wholly alike, but which suggest that they are sufficiently alike to class them together and contrast them not only with constitutional systems, but also with former types of autocracy. . . .

The basic features or traits which we suggest as generally recognized to be common to totalitarian dictatorships are six in number. The "syndrome," or pattern of interrelated traits, of the totalitarian dictatorship consists of an ideology, a single party typically led by one man, a terroristic police, a communications monopoly, a weapons monopoly, and a centrally directed economy. . . .

These six basic features, which we think constitute the character of totalitarian dictatorship, form a cluster of interrelated traits, intertwined and mutually supporting each other, as usual in "organic" systems. They should therefore not be considered in isolation or be made the focal point of comparisons, such as "Caesar developed a terroristic secret police, therefore he was the first totalitarian dictator," or "the Catholic Church has practised ideological thought control, therefore. . . ."

The totalitarian dictatorships all possess the following:

1. An official ideology, consisting of an official body of doctrine covering all vital aspects of man's existence to which everyone living in that society is supposed to adhere, at least passively; this ideology is characteristically focused and projected toward a perfect final state of mankind, that is to say, it contains a chilias-

tic claim, based upon a radical rejection of the existing society and conquest of the world for the new one.

2. A single mass party led typically by one man, the "dictator," and consisting of a relatively small percentage of the total population (up to 10 percent) of men and women, a hard core of them passionately and unquestioningly dedicated to the ideology and prepared to assist in every way in promoting its general acceptance, such a party being hierarchically, oligarchically organized, and typically either superior to, or completely intertwined with the bureaucratic government organization.

3. A system of terroristic police control, supporting but also supervising the party for its leaders, and characteristically directed not only against demonstrable "enemies" of the regime, but against arbitrarily selected classes of the population; the terror of the secret police systematically exploiting modern science, and more especially scientific psychology.

4. A technologically conditioned near-complete monopoly of control, in the hands of the party and its subservient cadres, of all means of effective mass communication, such as the press, radio, motion pictures.

5. A similarly technologically conditioned near-complete monopoly of control (in the same hands) of all means of effective armed combat.

6. A central control and direction of the entire economy through the bureaucratic coordination of its formerly independent corporate entities, typically including most other associations and group activities.

The enumeration of these six traits or trait clusters is not meant to suggest that there might not be others, now insufficiently recognized, but that these are universally acknowledged to be the features of totalitarian dictatorship to which the writings of students of the most varied backgrounds, including totalitarian writers, bear witness. . . .

Let us now turn to our first point, namely, that these systems are historically "unique"; that is to say, that no government like totalitarian dictatorship has ever before existed, even though it bears a resemblance to autocracies of the past. It may be interesting to consider briefly some data which show that the six traits we have just identified are to a large extent lacking in historically known autocratic regimes. Neither the Oriental despotisms of the more remote past, nor the absolute monarchies of modern Europe, neither the tyrannies of the ancient Greek cities, nor the Roman Empire, nor yet the tyrannies of the city-states of the Italian Renaissance and the Bonapartist military dictatorships of the last century exhibit this design, this combination of features, though they may possess one or another of its constituent traits. For example, efforts have often been made to organize some kind of secret police, but they have not been even horse-and-buggy affairs compared with the terror of the Gestapo or of the OGPU (MVD today). Similarly, there have been both military and propagandistic concentrations of power and control, but the limits of technology prevented any thoroughgoing development along totalitarian lines. It is very evident, we trust, that the six distinctive features here sketched, and to be developed in what follows, sharply differentiate contemporary totalitarian dictatorships from past autocratic regimes. Certainly neither the Roman emperor nor the absolute monarch sought or needed a party to support him nor an ideology in the modern party sense, and the same is obviously true of oriental despots. The tyrants of Greece and Italy may have had a party—that of the Medicis in Florence was called *lo stato*—but they had no ideology to speak of. And, of course, all of these autocratic regimes were far removed from the very distinctive features which are rooted in modern technology, from the terror to the centrally directed economy.

Something more should perhaps be added on the subject of technology. This technological aspect of totalitarianism is, of course, particularly striking in the matter of weapons and communications, but it is involved also in the secret police terror, depending as it does upon technically enhanced possibilities of supervision and control of the movement of persons. In addition, the centrally directed economy presupposes the reporting, cataloging, and calculating devices provided by modern technology. In short, four of the six traits are technologically conditioned. . . .

. . . With few exceptions, the trend of technological advance implies the trend toward greater and greater size of organization. In the perspective of these four traits, therefore, totalitarian societies appear to be merely exaggerations, but nonetheless logical exaggerations, of the technological state of modern society.

The same cannot be said with respect to the first two distinctive features of totalitarian dictatorships, for neither ideology nor party have any significant relation to the state of technology. (This may not be strictly true, since the mass conversion continually attempted by totalitarian propaganda through its effective use of the communications monopoly could not be carried through without it.) However, the party, its leader(s), and the ideology link the totalitarian dictatorship to modern democracy. It is the perversion of democracy. Not only did Hitler, Mussolini, and Lenin build typical parties within a constitutional, if not a democratic, context but the connection is plain between the stress on ideology and the role which platforms and other types of ideological goal-formation play in democratic parties. To be sure, totalitarian parties developed a pronounced authoritarian pattern while organizing themselves into effective revolutionary instruments of action; but, at the same time, its leaders, beginning with Marx and Engels, saw themselves as constituting the vanguard of the democratic movement of their day, and Stalin always talked of the Soviet totalitarian society as the "perfect democracy"; Hitler and Mussolini made similar statements. Both the world brotherhood of the proletariat and the folk community were conceived of as supplanting the class divisions of past societies by a complete harmony—the classless society of the socialist tradition.

Not only the party but also its ideology harkens back to the democratic context within which the totalitarian movements arose. Ideology generally, but more especially totalitarian ideology, involves a high degree of convictional certainty. As has been indicated, totalitarian ideology consists of an official doctrine which radically rejects the preexisting society in terms of a chiliastic proposal for a new one. As such it contains strongly utopian elements, some kind of notion of a paradise on earth. This utopian and chiliastic outlook of totalitarian ideologies gives them a pseudoreligious quality. In fact, they often elicit in the less critical followers a depth of conviction and a fervor of devotion usually found only among persons inspired by a transcendent faith. Whether these aspects of totalitarian ideologies bear some sort of relationship to the religions which they seek to replace is arguable. Marx denounced religion as "the opium of the people." It would seem that this is rather an appropriate way of describing totalitarian ideologies. In place of the more or less same platforms of regular political parties, critical of the existing state of affairs in a limited way, totalitarian ideologies are perversions of such programs. They substitute faith for reason, magic exhortation for scientific knowledge. And yet, it must be recognized that there is enough of these same elements in the operations of democratic parties to attest to the relation between them and their perverted descendants, the totalitarian movements. That is why these movements must be seen and analyzed in their relationship to the democracy which they seek to supplant.

In summary, these regimes could have arisen only within the context of mass democracy and modern technology. . . .

THE TOTALITARIAN DICTATOR

The reader may wonder why we do not discuss the "structure of government," or perhaps the "constitution" of these totalitarian systems. The reason is that these structures are of very little importance; they are continually changing, and they do so accordingly to the old French adage: "tout ça change, tout c'est la même chose." The "struture of government" has no real significance because the power of decision is completely concentrated, either in a single leader or in a collective body, at least for a limited period. More specifically, a constitution has, under these conditions, largely propagandistic value. It is not a constitution in the functional Western sense of providing a system of effective, regularized restraints, but a disguise by which a "democratic" framework is being suggested, a kind of window-dressing for the totalitarian reality. Such bodies of the Soviet Union and the several satellites as appear in the garb of "legislative bodies," or the Reichstag of Hitler's Germany, are essentially there to acclaim the decisions made. Similarly, the judicial machinery, devoid of all independence, is actually part and parcel of the administrative and bureaucratic hierarchy. The very shapelessness of the vast bureaucratic machinery is part of the technique of manipulating the absolute power which the dictator and his lieutenants have at their disposal. It is therefore necessary to say something more about these subleaders.

It is this significant role played in the totalitarian system by the political lieutenants of the dictator that suggests an additionally unique feature of the system. These political lieutenants wield the levers of control that hold the totalitarian dictatorship together, and are instrumental in maintaining the dictator in power. Yet in spite of this crucial function most studies of modern totalitarianisms tend to ignore the political phenomenon of the dictator's lieutenants. A notable exception to this is Sigmund Neumann's path-breaking *Permanent Revolution*. In it Neumann attempted the first analysis of the totalitarian lieutenant and pointed to the four decisive elements which "make up the composite structure of the leader's henchmen." These, he suggested, were the bureaucratic, feudal, democratic, and militant.

The bureaucratic element, in the light of this analysis, is the outstanding feature of the totalitarian leadership elite. Modern totalitarianism, unlike the more traditional dictatorships, is a highly bureaucratized system of power. Without this complex bureaucracy the total character of the system could not be maintained. The party organization in particular is a hierarchically structured political machine, and the efficient bureaucrat is an indispensable political lieutenant of the dictator. In this respect the similarity between such men as Bormann and Malenkov is more than striking—they were both capable and efficient bureaucrats who held their positions by virtue not only of administrative ability but, and this in totalitarianism is more important, "because they were found worthy of the supreme leader's confidence."

The feudal element, in terms of Neumann's analysis, is involved in the system of delegation of power to local satraps, be they *Gauleiters* or *Obkom* secretaries, who then act on behalf of the dictator. Such "feudal" vassals are not only territorially distributed; they also operate on the top levels, manipulating important levers of power such as the secret police. Himmler, Bocchini, and Beria were thus responsible for making sure that no internal challenge to the dictator's power arose, and the dictator at all times had to make certain that such posts were filled by men of unquestionable loyalty. In return, all of these lieutenants shared in the system of spoils, and every effort was made to develop in them a vested interest in the continued maintenance of the dictator's power.

The third feature of this leadership elite is its internal democratic element. That is not to say that it is subject to the customary democratic processes of selection and election. "Dictatorship is democracy for the insiders alone. Brutal and merciless as the lieutenants usually are toward their enemies, strutting like the gods of vengeance, they had better not play the boss within the circle of their associates." This is actually an oligarchic rather than a democratic equality. The lieutenants must accordingly be careful not to appear to crave excessive popularity. Such a craving can have disastrous effects also in so far as it may challenge the dictator's own domain. And the totalitarian dictator tolerates no trespassers on his power. The political lieutenants must thus limit themselves to the function of providing the dictator with the necessary contact with the masses and acting as his gauges of public opinion.

The final element, growing out of the revolutionary character of totalitarianism, is the militancy of the leadership. The political lieutenants must act as subleaders in the struggle for the achievement of the totalitarian society. Each in his particular sphere, the totalitarian lieutenant must attempt to break down all resistance to the implementation of the ideological-political goals of the regime. He must lead the "battle of the grain," or he must strive for higher accomplishments in "socialist competition." He may even have to encourage women to increase the number of their pregnancies. And it is through such battles, be they local or national, that the political lieutenants are weaned, steeled, and promoted. . . .

It is evident from the experience to date that totalitarian leadership is built upon metarational emotional appeals that are cast in strongly rational terms. The analysis of ideology will show that this leadership is believed to be an executioner of history, of forces that arise inevitably from the predestined course of social events. It is the consequent sense of mission that has led to the intrepretation of this leadership as charismatic. Such a view entirely overlooks that this "appeal" is reinforced by factors that are totally absent in the case of genuine charisma, more especially the control of mass communications and propaganda, and the terror apparatus. Both these features fully mature only in the course of the effective seizure of total power, but they are present from the start. . . .

There is no particular reason for inventing a weird term to designate this type of leadership, other than to say that it is "totalitarian." It represents a distinct and separate type, along with the "traditional," the "rational-legal," and the "charismatic." It may be helpful, considering the pseudo-religious emotionalism of these regimes, to designate this kind of totalitarian leadership as "pseudo-charismatic." It bears certain resemblances to still another distinct type, also not adequately developed by Weber and his followers, the "revolutionary" leader. Indeed, it may be argued that the "totalitarian" leader is a kind of "revolutionary" leader. Certainly, the characteristic features of Hitler or Stalin are more nearly comparable to those of Robespierre or Cromwell; but a detailed analysis would lead us too far afield.

In any case it might be said in conclusion and by way of a summary that the totalitarian leader possesses more nearly absolute power than any previous type of political leader, that he is completely identified with his actual following, both by himself and by them, in a kind of mystical union, that he is able to operate on both these levels as he does because he is backed by mass propaganda and terror—coercive cohesion—and that therefore his leadership is not to be confused either with tyranny, or despotism, or absolutism in their historical forms.

THE NATURE AND ROLE OF THE PARTY

. . . In the matured totalitarian society the role of the party is a distinctive one which bears little resemblance to the role of parties in democratic societies. As has been pointed out in the preceding chapter, it is the role of the party to provide a following for the dictator with which he can identify himself. According to a well-known phrase of Mussolini, the party has the function of the "capillaries" in the body; it is neither the heart, nor the head, but those endings where the blood of party doctrine, party policy, and party sentiment mingles with the rest of the body politic. In a sense, the party may be pictured as the "elite" of the totalitarian society, if the word elite is taken in a very neutral sense. In view of the total dependence of the party as a following upon the leader at its head, it can be argued that the party does not possess any corporate existence of its own. It is in this respect comparable to the Hobbesian state, in which all the separate members of the society are severally and totally dependent upon the sovereign. But somehow such a view seems not to do justice to the collective sense of the whole, and the almost complete loss of personal identity which the party members suffer, or rather enjoy, as they feel themselves merged in the larger whole. This feeling seems to contradict another aspect of these movements, namely, the unquestioning obedience. Fascists and Nazis never wearied of repeating Mussolini's formula: "Believe, Obey, Fight"—these were the focal points of fascist and Nazi education. In this kind of military subordination, the individual seems to confront the commander as an alien and wholly detached being. The answer to this seeming paradox, fascist writers found in what they conceived to be the "style" of the new life. This "style of living" was in Nazi Germany proclaimed, as it had been in Italy, to be that of the "marching column," it being indifferent for what purpose the column was being formed. . . .

Generally speaking, these facts show that the party and/or special cadres within it will be highly selective and elitist in a totalitarian dictatorship. This tendency toward elitism reinforces the strictly hierarchical structuring of the totalitarian parties we have noted above. The rigid hierarchy and centralized power are the result of an evolutionary process; everywhere there is at first considerable impact from below; later the party following becomes more and more subdued, until finally its influence is negligible. This is part of the maturing process of totalitarian regimes. Rotation of party leadership becomes a very real problem in connection with this solidifying of the hierarchy. Both in Italy and Germany, the fact that the same leader remained in control throughout the existence of the dictatorship undoubtedly inhibited such rotation. Yet, a purge occurred in both regimes by which some of the older subleaders were eliminated. Others would no doubt have followed after the war, if several confidential statements to that effect by Hitler,

Himmler, and others are allowed to stand. But such crises notwithstanding, the party constitutes the mainstay of totalitarian dictatorship. Without his party's support the dictator would be inconceivable; his unquestioned leadership gives the party its peculiar dynamic, indeed fanatical, devotion to the dictatorship, and the spineless attitude of subjection of its members toward the man at the top is merely the psychological counterpart to the party's ruthless assertion of the will and determination to rule and to shape the society in its image. . . .

THE HISTORICAL ROOTS OF TOTALITARIAN IDEOLOGY

In seeking to trace the roots of totalitarian ideology, every kind of link has been argued. Marx and Hegel, Nietzsche and Hobbes, Kant and Rousseau, Plato and Aristotle, St. Augustine, Luther, and Calvin—all have been charged with having forged the ideas that became weapons in the arsenal of the totalitarians. Since the thinkers thus involved are in turn related to many other intellectual trends and views, it is not too much to suggest that the sum of all the arguments is plainly this: totalitarian ideology is rooted in the totality of Western thought and more especially its political thought. To be sure, the key points of emphasis, such as equality, justice, freedom, are of so general a nature that they do not lend themselves to very precise analysis in this context. But even more specific points, like the stress on democracy or the state, are similarly elusive. This situation should not surprise anyone, for the programs of action which the totalitarians proclaim are programs cast in terms of the antecedent states of European and American society (with interesting variations introduced in cases such as China) and they must therefore be related to the patterns of ideas associated with these antecedent states. Moreover, since ideology has an instrumental function, as we have seen, totalitarian leaders will fashion their ideological tools to fit the states of mind of the masses they are addressing. For example the idea of progress, so peculiar a product of the Western mind, is embedded in the totalitarian thought so deeply that it would collapse if this idea were eliminated. . . .

The translation of an ideology into practice usually serves to reveal certain inadequacies inherent in human foresight. Attempts to picture the future and to prescribe the methods of achieving it clearly cannot conceive of all eventualities, of all possible situations, and communism is further handicapped by the general looseness of its philosophical structure. Consequently the schismatic movements which developed immediately as attempts were made to transform Marxism into political practice were, apart from pure power factors, the inevitable product of such an attempted implementation. When theory is applied to a real-life situation, there are usually only two alternatives: one is to modify theory so as to make it more compatible with the prerequisites of practice, and the other is to attempt to force reality to fit the theory. The totalitarians, by their almost complete rejection of the *status quo*, are inclined to attempt to force history to fit their conception of it. And when such a conception involves a far-reaching idea of the desirable, that is, historically inevitable, scheme of social organization, the efforts to mold society to fit it, and the consequent measures to break down the resistance to it, result in totalitarianism. . . .

It is noteworthy, however, that both communism and fascism are characterized by their insistence on the revolutionary fulfillment of the "truths" of their doctrines, and it is this insistence that leads to the further conclusions on the necessity of a disciplined party—the elite of the proletariat or of the nation. This party was to eliminate the remnants of the vanquished. Its infallible leadership, through "intuition" or "science," was to effect the conditions which, according to the ideology, are considered necessary for the achievement of its utopian apocalypse. It is precisely this attempt to impose on society a rationally, or rather pseudorationally, conceived pattern of distinctly novel forms of social organization that leads to the totalitarian oppression. And since this oppression is justified in terms of the ideology, this ideology is totalitarian. . . .

All in all, our discussion has shown that the roots of the totalitarian ideologies, both communist and fascist, are actually intertwined with the entire intellectual heritage of modern man, and that all specific links should be seen, not in terms of causation—of this or that thinker or group of thinkers being "responsible for" the totalitarian ideologies —but as strands of a complex and variegated tapestry. The specific totalitarian ingredient, namely, the employment, even glorification, of violence for the realization of the goals which the ideology posits, is largely absent from the thought of those whose ideas these ideologies have utilized, and, in utilizing them, distorted.

In the discussion of the role of ideology in totalitarian societies, some deny, as we noted, that ideology plays any significant part in the thinking of the leaders. Those who argue thus usually dwell upon the changes in ideology that they feel are in fact corruptions, proving the insincerity of the leaders. The key leadership groups are said not to take the ideology seriously, but to manipulate it, to change it arbitrarily to suit their shifting policy lines. But change need not be corruption; it can be genuine adaptation and meaningful change. It must, however, be admitted that in the case of Hitler, a strong case can be made for such a claim, because of Hitler's own cynical statements about the matter. Certainly, several well-known passages in Hitler's *Mein Kampf* as well as remarks reported by Rauschning in *The Revolution of Nihilism*, lend color to the proposition that Hitler's attitude toward ideology was "manipulative." On the other hand, Hitler's secret talks give a different impression, even though ideology does not play a decisive role; in these monologues Hitler clearly stays within the framework of his racist ideology.

Whatever may be the conclusions concerning Hitler's opinions, it appears quite clear that Soviet leadership, and Communist leadership generally, has continued to attach considerable importance to ideology. In spite of the vigorous denunciations of Trotskyite and other opposition elements, one is obliged to conclude that ideology plays a significant part in Soviet life, and that the leaders are sincerely exercised over ideological issues. All the ingenuity of the opposition has actually only been able to prove that there are important *changes* in the ideological pattern employed by the leaders. . . .

THE STAGES OF DEVELOPMENT AND THE FUTURE OF TOTALITARIAN DICTATORSHIP

In much of the foregoing discussion, there have been some implicit notions about the stages or phases of totalitarian development. From time to time, explicit statements have been made regarding them. At the very outset, we suggested that totalitarian dictatorship does not come into existence by a "seizure of power," as is assumed in so much of the literature regarding the subject. What is seized is the control of the existing government, customarily referred to as the state, and a dictatorship is set up in order to realize the totalitarian ideology of the party movement which has "seized the power." But the total transformation of the existing society that this ideology calls for quickly runs into numerous and formidable obstacles. The series of critical situations thus created give rise to the swift enlargement of power, and the totalitarian radicalization of the means of control; in the course of this process the totalitarian dictatorship comes into being.

In view of this gradual emergence of the totalitarian features of these dictatorships, it is evident that these totalitarian systems were not the result of intentional action. True, the total character of the ideology led to a dim appreciation of the difficulties, and a corresponding ideological acceptance of force and violence. The acceptance of violence also carried with it the acceptance of fraud, and more especially propagandistic fraud on a large scale, as a more special form of violence, namely, that done to mind and sentiment. But force, fraud, and violence have always been features of organized government, and they do not constitute by themselves the distinctive totalitarian operation. This operation we have defined in terms of a syndrome of interrelated traits or model features, the emergence of which signalizes the consummation of the totalitarian evolution. It is easy to identify these features, once they have come into full play: Italy, Germany, Russia—they all had emerged by about 1936 as totalitarian dictatorships; China and a considerable number of satellites have followed suit in the years since the Second World War. All these exhibit the six traits we have identified as characteristic: a total ideology, a single mass party, a terroristic secret police, a monopoly of mass communication, a monopoly of weapons, and a centrally directed planned economy.

The collapse of two of these totalitarian dictatorships occurred as a result of war and foreign invasion. If we study these wars, we find that they were the natural consequence of the ideologies of these particular dictatorships. Demonstrably, the ideologies themselves, with their glorification of violence, were at least in part responsible for the grave errors in judgment which launched the leadership into their belligerency. Other difficulties contributed to the defeat; some of these are once again definitely traceable to ideological and other defects of these regimes. More particularly the concentration of all power in a single man's hands, when combined with the absence of any sort of continuing critical evaluation of governmental operations, greatly enhanced the probability of erroneous judgments with fateful consequences.

But the end of these particular regimes, linked as they were to some specific features of their ideology, must not mislead one into readily assuming the early demise of totalitarianism. One need not go so far as to envision with George Orwell a world which in 1984 will be divided between three warring sets of totalitarians in order to appreciate the possibly lasting qualities of totalitarian dictatorship. More particularly the inroads of totalitarianism into the Orient, where despotic forms of government have been the rule for thousands of years, ought to give one pause, and prevent any too optimistic estimate of the totalitarians' lack of capacity for survival. We noted at the outset that autocratic regimes have often lasted for centuries, even when their oppressive practices became ever more pronounced. Therefore the mere maturing of the totalitarian autocracy into regularized patterns of organized violence need not spell their destruction; quite the contrary. Hence, since the end of totalitarian dictatorship is purely a matter of speculation to which we may return at the end of this discussion, let us start with its beginning.

As we just noted and indicated at various points in our study, the totalitarian dictatorship in our meaning of the term emerges some time after the seizure of power by the leaders of the movement that had developed in support of the ideology. The typical sequence is therefore that of ideology, movement, party, government. The point of time when the totalitarian government emerges may be reasonably fixed and delimited. It is that point at which the leadership sees itself obliged to employ open and legally unadorned violence for maintaining itself, most particularly against internal opposition due to ideological dissensions arising from within the movement's own ranks. In the Soviet Union, this point is marked by Stalin's liquidation of his erstwhile colleagues in the USSR's leadership and more particularly by his epochal struggle with Trotsky. In Nazi Germany, Hitler's bloody suppression of Roehm and his followers represents this totalitarian "breakthrough." In Mussolini's Italy, the Matteotti murder and its sequel are one turning point, the attack on Abyssinia another. In China, the totalitarian government seems to have emerged full-fledged, which is due to the fact that a kind of dictatorial government had been in existence for a considerable time prior to the Communists' establishment of control over all of China, namely, in those provinces that they had controlled and developed in their war against the Japanese. But even here, the true totalitarian maturation may be fixed at the point where the purge of any competitors to Mao Tse-Tung's absolute dictatorial control occurred. . . .

. . . The lack of a "model" had indeed been a striking feature of the development of totalitarian dictatorship in the Soviet Union, as we have stressed at the outset. The lack of such a model cannot be claimed with quite the same justification in the case of the fascists and Nazis; for while they doctrinally rejected the Soviet Union altogether, there is a good deal of evidence that they followed its example in a number of respects concerning vital features of the totalitarian system. When they instituted the secret police and the monopoly of propaganda, the corresponding transformation of education, and the organizing of the youth, and finally the central planning, and when they developed the technique of a rigidly hierarchical party apparatus, the fascists followed essentially Soviet models. To what extent this was a matter of conscious imitation does not seem very important, since these features are inherent in the dynamics of the totalitarian movement. It may, however, be well to trace this "phasing" through some of its distinctive component fields, more especially ideology, party, and secret police. This sketch provides a summary of what has been discussed in greater detail before.

We saw when discussing ideology that the radical change which a totalitarian ideology demands necessarily occasions adjustments and adaptations to reality and its situational needs when an attempt is made to "realize" such an ideology. The totalitarian revolutionaries are, in this respect, in no different situation than have been other revolutionaries before them. In the French revolution, especially, the violent controversies over the ideological "meaning" of the revolution led to the *Terreur*. But since the ideology lacked that pseudoscientific ingredient which has enabled the communist and fascist totalitarians to insist on the "mercilessness of the dialectics" (Stalin) and the "ice-cold reasoning" (Hitler), a totalitarian ideology did not develop. Whether its exponents are convinced or merely pretending, the totalitarian ideology requires that it be maintained even while it is being "corrupted." It is at this point, when the inner contradictions of the totalitarian ideology become evident, that the totalitarian breakthrough occurs. For since there is no longer any possibility of maintaining the logicality of the ideology on logical grounds, total violence must be deployed in order to do so.

In the development of the party, which is closely related to this ideological evolution, an analogous process takes place. In the original movement, when the party fights for success against a hostile environment, all the leader's authority, or a very large part of it, springs from the genuine comradeship which unites the effective participants. After the seizure of power, this relationship continues to operate, but—due to the new situation confronting the leadership with the vast tasks of a government that aspires to accomplish a total change and reconstruction of society—it becomes rapidly bureaucratized. Not only the government but the party is transformed into an increasingly formalized hierarchy. As is always the case, the *apparat* acquires its own weight and operates according to its inherent laws of large-scale bureaucracy. At the point of the totalitarian breakthrough, purges of former "comrades" reveal that it is no longer a matter of "belonging" to a movement, but one of submission to autocratic decisions which determine a person's right to belong to the party.

Hand in hand with this development goes that of the secret police. In order to become the instrument of total terror which the police system is in a matured totalitarian system, it must acquire the requisite knowledge of its human material, the potential victims of its terroristic activity. Centers of possible opposition have to be identified, techniques of espionage and counterespionage have to be developed, courts and similar judicial procedures of an nontotalitarian past have to be subjected to effective control. Experience and observation show that the time required for these tasks varies. In the Soviet Union, the tsarist secret police provided a ready starting point, and hence the Soviets got under way in this field with their Cheka very quickly. The entrenched liberal tradition in Italy allowed the fascists to organize the secret police effectively only in 1926, and it took another two years before it really "got hold" of the situation. The Nazis, although anxious to clamp down at once, did not perfect their secret police system until well after the Blood Purge of 1934, when Himmler first emerged as the key figure in the manipulation of this essential totalitarian ingredient.

It is at the point at which the totalitarian breakthrough occurs that the total planning of the economy imposes itself. For it is at this point that the social life of the society has become so largely disorganized that nothing short of central direction will do. In a sense, this total planning is the sign of the culmination of the process. In Soviet Russia, it is the year 1928, in Nazi Germany that of 1936, while in Italy it comes with the instituting of the corporative set-up in 1934 (it had been grandiloquently announced in 1930), though perhaps the Ethiopian war was even more decisive. . . .

What then is going to be the course of totalitarian development? If one extrapolates from the past course of evolution, it seems most likely that the totalitarian dictatorships will continue to become more total, even though the rate of intensification may slow down. This view is questioned by those who expect the requirements of the bureaucratic organization to assert themselves and to lead to a less violent form of autocratic regime. In this connection, it is argued that the technological needs of an advancing industrial civilization will also play a decisive role. There is the possibility here of an inherent conflict between industrialization and totalitarian dictatorship, through the rise of a class of managers and technicians, who, when they allied themselves with the military, might wish to abandon the ideology and the party and thus bring the totalitarian dictatorship to an end. This development is conceivable, but not very likely. It may be doubted that such managers and technicians have any imaginable conception of the ground upon which the legitimacy and hence the authority of their continuing power might be built. . . .

Whether it is possible, in terms of a developmental construct, to forecast the probable course of totalitarian evolution seems more doubtful. We prefer the simple extrapolation of recent trends, and the estimate of broader potentials in terms of long-range observation of autocratic regimes throughout history. Considered in such terms, the prospect of totalitarian dictatorship seems unclear. Leaving aside the possibility of liquidation by war, there might conceivably be internal transformation. "It is possible," as one highly qualified observer said, "that the 'wave' of totalitarianism has reached its high water mark. And it may well be that in the not too distant future it will start rolling back." It may be. But if one such totalitarianism disappeared, others may appear to take its place, due to the endemic conditions which have given rise to them. Totalitarian dictatorship, a novel form of autocracy, more inimical to human dignity than autocracies in the past, appears to be a highly dynamic form of government which is still in the process of evolving. Whether it will, in the long run, prove to be a viable form of social and political organization remains to be seen. Nonetheless, large portions of mankind may have to pass through is crucible, before becoming ready, if they survive the ordeal, for more complex forms of political organization.

Hannah Arendt

FASCISM AS TOTALITARIANISM:
IDEOLOGY AND TERROR

Hannah Arendt (b. Hanover, Germany, 1906) is perhaps the most distinguished student of the eminent Swiss philosopher-historian Karl Jaspers. She fled the Nazi regime in 1933 and eventually migrated to the United States in 1941. Arendt is convinced that our times have a unique significance in human history. As a result she has devoted her intellectual efforts toward an understanding of some of the most vast and incomprehensible problems of modern history.

In the preceding chapters we emphasized repeatedly that the means of total domination are not only more drastic but that totalitarianism differs essentially from other forms of political oppression known to us, such as despotism, tyranny, and dictatorship. Wherever it rose to power, it developed entirely new political institutions and destroyed all social, legal, and political traditions of the country. No matter what the specifically national tradition or the particular spiritual source of its ideology, totalitarian government always transformed classes into masses, supplanted the party system, not by one-party dictatorships, but by a mass movement, shifted the center of power from the army to the police, and established a foreign policy openly directed toward world domination. Present totalitarian governments have developed from one-party systems; whenever these became truly totalitarian, they started to operate according to a system of values so radically different from all others, that none of our traditional legal, moral, or common sense utilitarian categories could any longer help us to come to terms with, or judge, or predict their course of action.

If it is true that the elements of totalitarianism can be found by re-tracing the history and analyzing the political implications of what we usually call the crisis of our century, then the conclusion is unavoidable that this crisis is no mere threat from the outside, no mere result of some aggressive foreign policy of either Germany or Russia, and that it will no more disappear with the death of Stalin than it disappeared with the fall of Nazi Germany. It may even be that the true predicaments of our time will assume their authentic form—though not necessarily the cruelest—only when totalitarianism has become a thing of the past.

It is in the line of such reflections to raise the question whether totalitarian government, born of this crisis and at the same time its clearest and only unequivocal symptom, is merely a makeshift arrangement, which borrows its methods of intimidation, its means of organization and its instruments of violence from the well-known political arsenal of tyranny, despotism, and dictatorships, and owes its existence only to the deplorable, but perhaps accidental failure of the traditional political forces—liberal or conservative, national or socialist, republican or mon-archist, authoritarian or democratic. Or whether, on the contrary, there is such a thing as the *nature* of totalitarian government, whether it has its own essence and can be compared with and defined like other forms of government such as Western thought has known and recognized since the times of ancient philosophy. If this is true, then the entirely new and unprecedented forms of totalitarian organization and course of action must rest on one of the few basic experiences which men can have whenever they live together, and are concerned with public affairs. If there is a basic experience which finds its political expression in totalitarian domination, then, in view of the novelty of the totalitarian form of government, this must be an experience which, for whatever reason, has never before served as the foundation of a body politic and whose general mood—although it may be familiar in every other respect —never before has pervaded, and directed the handling of, public affairs.

If we consider this in terms of the history of ideas, it seems extremely unlikely. For the forms of government under which men live have been very few; they were discovered early, classified by the Greeks, and have proved extraordinarily long-lived. If we apply these findings, whose fundamental idea, despite many variations, did not change in the two and a half thousand years that separate Plato from Kant, we are tempted at once to interpret totalitarianism as some modern form of tyranny, that is a lawless government where power is wielded by one man. Arbi-trary power, unrestricted by law, wielded in the interest of the ruler and hostile to the interests of the governed, on one hand, fear as the principle of action, namely fear of the people by the ruler and fear of the ruler by the people, on the other—these have been the hallmarks of tyranny throughout our tradition.

Instead of saying that totalitarian government is unprecedented, we could also say that it has exploded the very alternative on which all definitions of the essence of governments have been based in political philosophy, that is the alternative between lawful and lawless government, between arbitrary and legitimate power. That lawful government and legitiment power, on one side, lawlessness and arbitrary power on the other, belonged together and were inseparable has never been questioned. Yet, totalitarian rule confronts us with a totally different kind of government. It defies, it is true, all positive laws, even to the extreme of defying those which it has itself established (as in the case of the Soviet Constitution of 1936, to quote only the most outstanding example) or which it did not care to abolish (as in the case of the Weimar Constitution which the Nazi government never revoked). But it operates neither without guidance of law nor is it arbitrary, for it claims to obey strictly and unequivocally those laws of Nature or of History from which all positive laws always have been supposed to spring. . . .

In the interpretation of totalitarianism, all laws have become laws of movement. When the Nazis talked about the law of nature or when the Bolsheviks talk about the law of history, neither nature nor history is any longer the stabilizing source of authority for the actions of mortal men; they are movements in themselves. Underlying the Nazis' belief in race laws as the expression of the law of nature in man is Darwin's idea of man as the product of a natural development which does not necessarily stop with the present species of human beings, just as under the Bolsheviks' belief in class-struggle as the expression of the law of history lies Marx's notion of society as the product of gigantic historical movement which races according to its own law of motion to the end of historical times when it will abolish itself.

The difference between Marx's historical and Darwin's naturalistic approach has frequently been pointed out, usually and rightly in favor of Marx. This has led us to forget the great and positive interest Marx took in Darwin's theories; Engels could not think of a greater compliment to Marx's scholarly achievements than to call him the "Darwin of history." If one considers, not the actual achievement, but the basic philosophies of both men, it turns out that ultimately the movement of history and the movement of nature are one and the same. Darwin's introduction of the concept of development into nature, his insistence that, at least in the field of biology, natural movement is not circular but unilinear, moving in an infinitely progressing direction, means in fact that nature is, as it were, being swept into history, that natural life is considered to be historical. The "natural" law of the survival of the fittest is just as much a historical law and could be used as such by racism as Marx's law of the survival of the most progressive class. Marx's class struggle, on the other hand, as the driving force of history, is only the outward expression of the development of productive forces which in turn have their origin in the "labor-power" of men. Labor, according to Marx, is not a historical but a natural-biological force—released through man's "metabolism with nature" by which he conserves his individual life and reproduces the species. Engels saw the affinity between the basic convictions of the two men very clearly because he understood the decisive role which the concept of development played in both theories. The tremendous intellectual change which took place in the middle of the last century consisted in the refusal to view or accept anything "as it is" and in the consistent interpretation of everything as being only a stage of some further development. Whether the driving force of this development was called nature or history is relatively secondary. In these ideologies, the term "law" itself changed its meaning: from expressing the framework of stability within which human actions and motions can take place, it became the expression of the motion itself. . . .

By lawful government we understand a body politic in which positive laws are needed to translate and realize the immutable *ius naturale* or the eternal commandments of God into standards of right and wrong. Only in these standards, in the body of positive laws of each country, do the *ius naturale* or the Commandments of God achieve their political reality. In the body politic of totalitarian government, this place of positive laws is taken by total terror, which is designed to translate into reality the law of movement of history or nature. Just as positive laws, though they define transgressions, are independent of them—the absence of crimes in any society does not render laws superfluous but, on the contrary, signifies their most perfect rule—so terror in totalitarian government has ceased to be a mere means for the suppression of opposition, though it is also used for such purposes. Terror becomes total when it becomes independent of all opposition; it rules supreme when nobody any longer stands in its way. If lawfulness is the essence of nontyrannical government and lawlessness is the essence of tyranny, then terror is the essence of totalitarian domination.

Terror is the realization of the law of movement; its chief aim is to make it possible for the force of nature or of history to race freely through mankind, unhindered by any spontaneous human action. As such, terror seeks to "stabilize" men in order to liberate the forces of nature or history. It is this movement which singles out the foes of mankind against whom terror is let loose, and no free action of either opposition or sympathy can be permitted to interfere with the elimination of the "objective enemy" of History or Nature, of the class or the race. Guilt and innocence become senseless notions; "guilty" is he who stands in the way of the natural or historical process which has passed judgment over "inferior races," over individuals "unfit to live," over "dying classes and decadent peoples." Terror executes these judgments, and before its court, all concerned are subjectively innocent: the murdered because they did nothing against the system, and the murderers because they do not really murder but execute a death sentence pronounced by some higher tribunal. The rulers themselves do not claim to be just or wise, but only to execute historical or natural laws; they do not apply laws, but execute a movement in accordance with its inherent law. Terror is lawfulness, if law is the law of the movement of some suprahuman force, Nature or History.

Terror as the execution of a law of movement whose ultimate goal is not the welfare of men or the interest of one man but the fabrication of mankind, eliminates individuals for the sake of the species, sacrifices the "parts" for the sake of the "whole." The suprahuman force of Nature or History has its own beginning and its own end, so that it can be hindered only by the new beginning and the individual end which the life of each man actually is. . . .

Total terror, the essence of totalitarian government, exists neither for nor against men. It is supposed to provide the forces of nature or history with an incomparable instrument to accelerate their movement. This movement, proceeding according to its own law, cannot in the long run be hindered; eventually its force will always prove more powerful than the most powerful forces engendered by the actions and the will of men. But it can be slowed down and is slowed down almost inevitably by the freedom of man, which even totalitarian rulers cannot deny, for this freedom—irrelevant and arbitrary as they may deem it—is identical with the fact that men are being born and that therefore each of them *is* a new beginning, begins, in a sense, the world anew. From the totalitarian point of view, the fact that men are born and die can be only regarded as an annoying interference with higher forces. Terror, therefore, as the obedient servant of natural or historical movement has to eliminate from the process not only freedom in any specific sense, but the very source of freedom which is given with the fact of the birth of man and resides in his capacity to make a new beginning. In the iron band of terror, which destroys the plurality of men and makes out of many the One who unfailingly will act as though he himself were part of the course of history or nature, a device has been found not only to liberate the historical and natural forces, but to accelerate them to a speed they never would reach if left to themselves. Practically speaking, this means that terror executes on the spot the death sentences which Nature is supposed to have pronounced on races or individuals who are "unfit to live," or History on "dying classes," without waiting for the slower and less efficient processes of nature or history themselves. . . .

In a perfect totalitarian government, where all men have become One Man, where all action aims at the acceleration of the movement of nature or history, where every single act is the execution of a death sentence which Nature or History has already pronounced, that is, under conditions where terror can be completely relied upon to keep the movement in constant motion, no principle of action separate from its essence would be needed at all. Yet as long as totalitarian rule has not conquered the earth and with the iron band of terror made each single man a part of one mankind, terror in its double function as essence of government and principle, not of action, but of motion, can not be fully realized. Just as lawfulness in constitutional government is insufficient to inspire and guide men's actions, so terror in totalitarian government is not sufficient to inspire and guide human behavior.

While under present conditions totalitarian domination still shares with other forms of government the need for a guide for the behavior of its citizens in public affairs, it does not need and could not even use a principle of action strictly speaking, since it will eliminate precisely the capacity of man to act. Under conditions of total terror not even fear can any longer serve as an advisor of how to behave, because terror chooses its victims without reference to individual actions or thoughts, exclusively in accordance with the objective necessity of the natural or historical process. Under totalitarian conditions, fear probably is more widespread than ever before; but fear has lost its practical usefulness when actions guided by it can no longer help to avoid the dangers man fears. The same is true for sympathy or support of the regime; for total terror not only selects its victims according to objective standards; it chooses its executioners with as complete a disregard as possible for the candidate's conviction and sympathies. The consistent elimination of conviction as a motive for action has become a matter of record since the great purges in Soviet Russia and the satellite countries. The aim of totalitarian education has never been to instill convictions but to destroy the capacity to form any. The introduction of purely objective criteria into the selective system of the SS troops was Himmler's great organizational invention; he selected the candidates from photographs according to purely racial criteria. Nature itself decided, not only who was to be eliminated, but also who was to be trained as an executioner.

No guiding principle of behavior, taken itself from the realm of human action, such as virtue, honor, fear, is necessary or can be useful to set into motion a body politic which no longer uses terror as a means of intimidation, but whose essence *is* terror. In its stead, it has introduced an entirely new principle into public affairs that dispenses with human will to action altogether and appeals to the craving need for some insight into the law of movement according to which the terror functions and upon which, therefore, all private destinies depend.

The inhabitants of a totalitarian country are thrown into and caught in the process of nature or history for the sake of accelerating its movement; as such, they can only be executioners or victims of its inherent law. The process may decide that those who today eliminate races and individuals or the members of dying classes and decadent peoples are tomorrow those who must be sacrificed. What totalitarian rule needs to guide the behavior of its subjects is a preparation to fit each of them equally well for the role of executioner and the role of victim. . . .

The question we raised at the start of these considerations and to which we know return is what kind of basic experience in the living-together of men permeates a form of government whose essence is terror and whose principle of action is the logicality of ideological thinking. That such a combination was never used before in the varied forms of political domination is obvious. Still, the basic experience on which it rests must be human and known to men, insofar as even this most "original" of all political bodies has been devised by, and is somehow answering the needs of, men.

It has frequently been observed that terror can rule absolutely only over men who are isolated against each other and that, therefore, one of the primary concerns of all tyrannical government is to bring this isolation about. Isolation may be the beginning of terror; it certainly is its most fertile ground; it always is its result. This isolation is, as it were, pretotalitarian; its hallmark is impotence insofar as power always comes from men acting together, "acting in concert" (Burke); isolated men are powerless by definition.

Isolation and impotence, that is the fundamental inability to act at all, have always been characteristic of tyrannies. Political contacts between men are severed in tyrannical government and the human capacities for action and power are frustrated. But not all contacts between men are broken and not all human capacities destroyed. The whole sphere of private life with the capacities for experience, fabrication, and thought are left intact. We know that the iron band of total terror leaves no space for such private life and that the self-coercion of totalitarian logic destroys man's capacity for experience and thought just as certainly as his capacity for action. . . .

. . . Totalitarian government, like all tyrannies, certainly could not exist without destroying the public realm of life, that is, without destroying, by isolating men, their political capacities. But totalitarian domination as a form of government is new in that it is not content with this isolation and destroys private life as well. It bases itself on loneliness, on the experience of not belonging to the world at all, which is among the most radical and desperate experiences of man.

Loneliness, the common ground for terror, the essence of totalitarian government, and for ideology or logicality, the preparation of its executioners and victims, is closely connected with uprootedness and superfluousness which have been the curse of modern masses since the beginning of the industrial revolution and have become acute with the rise of imperialism at the end of the last century and the breakdown of political institutions and social traditions in our own time. To be uprooted means to have no place in the world, recognized and guaranteed by others; to be superfluous means not to belong to the world at all. . . .

What prepares men for totalitarian domination in the nontotalitarian world is the fact that loneliness, once a borderline experience usually suffered in certain marginal social conditions like old age, has become an everyday experience of the evergrowing masses of our century. The merciless process into which totalitarianism drives and organizes the masses looks like a suicidal escape from this reality. The "ice-cold reasoning" and the "mighty tentacle" of dialectics which "seizes you as in a vise" appears like a last support in a world where nobody is reliable and nothing can be relied upon. It is the inner coercion whose only content is the strict avoidance of contradictions that seems to confirm a man's identity outside all relationships with others. It fits him into the iron band of terror even when he is alone, and totalitarian domination tries never to leave him alone except in the extreme situation of solitary confinement. By destroying all space between men and pressing men against each other, even the productive potentialities of isolation are annihilated; by teaching and glorifying the logical reasoning of loneliness where man knows that he will be utterly lost if ever he lets go of the first premise from which the whole process is being started, even the slim chances that loneliness may be transformed into solitude and logic into thought are obliterated. If this practice is compared with that of tyranny, it seems as if a way had been found to set the desert itself in motion, to let loose a sand storm that could cover all parts of the inhabited earth.

The conditions under which we exist today in the field of politics are indeed threatened by these devastating sand storms. Their danger is not that they might establish a permanent world. Totalitarian domination, like tyranny, bears the germs of its own destruction. Just as fear and the impotence from which fear springs are antipolitical principles and throw men into a situation contrary to political action, so loneliness and the logical-ideological deducing the worst that comes from it represent an antisocial situation and harbor a principle destructive for all human living-together. Nevertheless, organized loneliness is considerably more dangerous than the unorganized impotence of all those who are ruled by the tyrannical and arbitrary will of a single man. Its danger is that it threatens to ravage the world as we know it—a world which everywhere seems to have come to an end—before a new beginning rising from this end has had time to assert itself.

Apart from such considerations—which as predictions are of little avail and less consolation—there remains the fact that the crisis of our time and its central experience have brought forth an entirely new form of government which as a potentiality and an everpresent danger is only too likely to stay with us from now on, just as other forms of government which came about at different historical moments and rested on different fundamental experiences have stayed with mankind regardless of temporary defeats—monarchies, and republics, tyrannies, dictatorships, and despotism.

But there remains also the truth that every end in history necessarily contains a new beginning; this beginning is the promise, the only "message" which the end can ever produce. Beginning, before it becomes a historical event, is the supreme capacity of man; politically, it is identical with man's freedom. *Initium ut esset homo creatus est*—"that a beginning be made man was created" said Augustine. This beginning is guaranteed by each new birth; it is indeed every man.

FASCISM AS A RADICAL FORM OF TRADITIONAL POLITICAL PROTEST

Eugen Weber

FASCISM AS THE CONJUNCTION OF RIGHT AND LEFT

Eugen Weber (b. Bucarest, Rumania, 1925) was educated in France and England before coming to the United States in 1955. He is the author of numerous articles and books on right-wing movements in France and Europe, including the authoritative work on Action Française. *He is presently Professor of History at the University of California, Los Angeles.*

Origins. The nineteenth century had seen the heyday of liberalism, the rise of parliamentary and democratic institutions, the affirmation of private enterprise and individual liberty. The twentieth century would be dominated by tendencies—collectivistic, authoritarian, antiparliamentary, and antidemocratic—which stressed elitism against equality, activism and irrationalism against reason and contract, the organic community against the constitutional society.

All these tendencies had their roots in the nineteenth century, and even earlier—in the organic nationalism of a Rousseau for whom the national body, made up of the dead, the living, and those as yet unborn, ideally obeyed a general will best defined as a special revelation, in the thought of Hegel, for whom the divine purpose revealed itself progressively in the history of nations; and in the romantic affirmation of the

From Eugen Weber, Varieties of Fascism (*Princeton, N.J.: Van Nostrand, 1964*), *pp. 7–17, 22–25, 139–43. Copyright 1964 by Eugen Weber. By permission of D. Van Nostrand Co., Inc.*

primacy of subjective passions, of instincts, and of will, by which man was supposed to come nearest to nature, to reality, and to expressing his true self.

Forgotten for a time or, better still, adapted to the passion for science, positive knowledge, and rational activity which reigned over the century —especially over its second half—these concepts were revived in the 1890s and the early 1900s, when political and scientific disillusions swung the pendulum away from rationalism, away from the individualistic liberalism of the enfranchised, constitution-minded, free-trading middle classes. The prosperous, respectable, law-abiding bourgeoisie was decadent and corrupt, proclaimed Friedrich Nietzsche (1844–1900); only dynamic men, ruthless in thought and action, could save the race. Instincts are stronger than reason and closer to reality, suggested Henri Bergson (1859–1941). The individual is a product of the clan, taught the sociologist Emile Durkheim (1858–1917); collective consciousness has its own existence, prior to individual consciousness. And while these simplified ideas percolated from their books and lectures to a vaster public, new generations whom reigning rationalism bored stood by to welcome them. It was at this time that many of the ideas and institutions of the nineteenth century took a new shape and sometimes a new direction, their function and meaning changing here and there to answer the needs of another age.

Nationalism and socialism had both been born or weaned in the nineteenth century. They were to be reaffirmed in the twentieth, but in forms less humanitarian and less liberal and for motives different from their original ones. Both nationalism and socialism had first appeared as liberating movements. In the shape they assumed during the 1900s, they would be less liberating than constricting. Where once they had expressed the real needs and real resentments of men oppressed, exploited, and insecure, now they were tapped as myths—potentially powerful invocations addressed to tendencies and awarenesses that they themselves had been instrumental in creating over the past century. And, while we know that both nationalism and socialism were potent as separate—generally antagonistic—creeds, both also contributed to those new phenomena peculiar to our age that we call fascism or National Socialism.

Neither fascism nor National Socialism has been investigated thoroughly, although both are highly characteristic of our time: a time in which theory and activism, pragmatic violence, and idealistic ruthlessness masquerading as positivism dominate or threaten all societies. The peculiar combination of nationalism and socialism seems to answer the needs of a great many states, even though this is not always explicitly acknowledged or self-conscious.

The study of fascist and National Socialist phenomena has suffered from several serious drawbacks: both movements expressed themselves in actions and statements which repelled serious scholars as they repelled any humane person; both movements were defeated in circumstances which make an unprejudiced approach difficult; and both movements, once defeated, were temporarily dismissed as having no further immediate significance, except of a purely historical order—and that could wait. Meanwhile, the fiery trail of fascism and Nazism, driving like destructive comets through Italian and German history, had drawn all eyes to these two countries, leaving little attention for similar phenomena elsewhere.

Because neither fascism nor National Socialism has been thoroughly analyzed, we lack sound definitions of either and frequently confuse the two. Only the ignorant still think that socialism and communism, much though they have in common, are one and the same thing. But even serious scholars are liable to refer to "German fascism," and to use fascism and National Socialism interchangeably. True, the activity of German National Socialists involved the violent methods which we associate with fascism; but violence is not the prerogative of either of these movements, and we shall see that there are fundamental differences between them which might help us to reach a new classification.

Today, terms like Nazi or fascist, especially the latter, have become adjectives used in a sense that is only vaguely descriptive and generally pejorative. Their purpose is often to give a dog a bad name, their use seldom exact: Franco is a fascist, Perón was a fascist, Pétain was a fascist, but Churchill, Eisenhower, and de Gaulle may be fascists too (depending upon who is talking), and so may Tito. Yet these phenomena, crucial to our time, are not only part of the history of the past, but of the present and the future as well. Fascism and National Socialism have to be analyzed and defined so as to establish in what they are alike and in what they differ, to discover what makes them start and what makes them tick, to understand to whom they appeal, why, and by what means.

Theory and Practice. There are two levels on which political ideas and political movements operate: theory and practice. Although we have been fascinated by fascist practice in Italy and Nazi practice under Hitler, we have paid relatively little attention to their theory and even less to evidence from other countries where similar movements and similar doctrines flourished. And yet the essence of certain doctrines is to be found in their expression when they have not yet "arrived": in the period of formulation, controversy, soapbox oratory, and obscure pamphleteering; in the discussions and exegeses of the movement's theorists, whose definitions and formulas may be removed from the brutal realities of the political struggle, but are accepted—and honored in the breach if not in the observance. The struggle to reach or to maintain power involves a political movement in hedging, compromise, back-pedaling, and all the complications which follow when theory has to be connected with practice, when it has to be adapted to the concrete realities of traditional politics and political maneuver. It is the theories, the doctrines, the ideologies of fascism and National Socialism—and the attempts to carry these into practice—that will be considered in the following pages.

It has been held that National Socialist doctrine is of no importance, because Hitler came to power in spite of it and, once in power, did not apply it—at least, not the socialist part. This kind of argument does not prevent us from studying Marxist or Leninist doctrine, even though the Bolshevik revolution of 1917 went counter to then-existing theories, and though Bolshevik practice since that time has only partially conformed to it. The aspect of communism changes according to whether it is practiced by Russians, Serbo-Croats, or Chinese; but we can study the theory of communism and learn a good deal from it. . . .

The argument is current that Fascist manifestoes or the program of the National Socialist German Workers' Party are meaningless because they were never really carried out. In fact, such statements were acted upon to quite a surprising extent. Even if they had not been, we should still learn a good deal by examining them, especially if we compare them to similar programs or doctrines evolved by movements in other countries and, perhaps, in other circumstances.

Earlier Movements. Movements of a National Socialist nature are not peculiar to the twentieth century. F. L. Schumann, in his book *The Nazi Dictatorship* (New York, 1935), suggests that the idea, if not the name, can be traced back to the German Romantics, to the autarkic economist Friedrich List (1789–1846), and also to Ferdinand Lassalle (1825–1864), the German-Jewish Socialist leader who was a contemporary of Bismarck. Fifteen years before Schumann's study, in a book published just after the First World War, *Prussianism and Socialism,* Oswald Spengler had argued that the prototype of the modern socialist state is to be found in the ideas of Frederick the Great, founder of the perfected Prussian bureaucracy. It is equally possible to trace the pattern of the planned totalitarian society back to Plato's *Republic,* and the fascist mentality to the turbulent, unscrupulous Callicles who appears in another Platonic dialogue, *Gorgias.*

Even if we try to narrow things down, we shall find self-asserted National Socialists rampant as far back as seventy years ago. In 1896,

Friedrich Naumann (1860–1919), the great economist of the Wilhelmian era, tried to organize what he called a National-Social Party. Something like it already existed in Austria, where it was called the German Workers' Party and where, in 1896, its leader Karl Lueger became Mayor of Vienna, a position he retained until 1910. During this time he carried out what by all accounts was a most thorough and efficient program of municipal socialism and also provided the basic inspiration of a young drifter called Adolf Hitler (1889–1945), who sometimes sold the party paper in the street. In 1918, Lueger's movement would change its name to the German National Socialist Party.

In France, meanwhile, in the same year that Lueger became Mayor of Vienna, a typical nationalist buccaneer was being given a lavish funeral in the Cathedral of Notre Dame, with the Archbishop of Paris officiating and Maurice Barrès, in his funeral oration, asserting that the Marquis de Morès, whose memory they had gathered to honor, had been both nationalist and socialist. As for himself, said Barrès (1862–1923), he also liked to insist on the intimate union of nationalist and socialist ideas.

Barrès had already expressed this view in a periodical, *La Cocarde*, where extreme nationalists collaborated with extreme syndicalists. The review only lasted from 1894 to 1895, but while it lasted, it preached the gospel of social revolution "whose accomplishment no power can henceforth prevent," it lambasted the established order, and it attacked with particular vigor the capitalist system that throve upon it. One of Barrès's admirers considered that the review "was exactly socialist in that it led a relentless struggle against economic liberalism, and called for the organization of labor and the suppression of the proletariat, that is to say its integration in society." This is not what most socialists would recognize as socialism, but there are a great many variants of socialism, and we shall see that this is the one which fascists and National Socialists favor. It was this that Barrès himself had in mind; and when in 1898 he stood for election in Nancy, capital of his native Lorraine, his program was headed "Nationalism, Protectionism, and Socialism," and his supporters gathered in the Republican Socialist Nationalist Committee.

They did not get very far; but the label was attractive. It was revived a few years later by Pierre Biétry, a dissident trade-union leader who tried to gather in a Socialist National Party the working-class opposition to the doctrinaire policies of the French Confederation of Labor (C.G.T.). Meanwhile, the idea itself was bringing young intellectuals together in a number of groups and reviews in which the nationalist disciples of Charles Maurras (1868–1952) worked together with the revolutionary syndicalist disciples of Georges Sorel (1857–1922). Maurras, a convinced royalist, had built up a movement—the *Action Française*—whose purpose was to restore the monarchy, a sense of order, hierarchy, and discipline in French political and intellectual life. Sorel, on the other hand, who came from the Republican left, was seeking to renovate current social revolutionary ideas and adapt them to the conditions of the twentieth century. At first sight, no more different points of view could be conceived. Both men, however, agreed in their criticism of the existing political, economic, and social order, of parliaments, democracy, liberalism, and capitalism, and both despised the existing parties of the right and left and their leadership for their conservative, stick-in-the-mud policies.

The brief flirtation did not go far, and its inspiration finally foundered in the great war (1914–18) in which most of the young enthusiasts lost their lives. But it represented a tendency, perhaps a need, which has persisted until our own day. In the next thirty years, more than a score of groups and movements appeared in France alone, bearing titles like National Syndicalists, Monarchist Socialists. National Proletarians, Revolutionary Patriots, or simply National Socialists.

Even if we consider that the combination of these supposedly antagonistic ideologies amounted to little, in movements that were often insignificant and generally short-lived, the question remains why people should be so interested in the conjunction of nationalism and socialism as to go on suggesting it, and what it was that made this conjunction seem relevant to so many about this time. The hint of an answer may be found in Clouard's words about the *Cocarde's* "relentless struggle against economic liberalism."

Antiliberalism. All opposition movements of the twentieth century seem to have in common this opposition to a liberalism defined on the economic plane as the application of competitive laissez-faire and on the political plane as the individualistic counterpart of laissez-faire which allows *particular* interests to assert themselves at the expense of the social whole. In opposing individualism and the apparently chaotic conclusions of private enterprise, their critics rediscover collectivism. On such grounds, they find that they have more in common with socialists (though not with Social-Democrats) than with more conservative groups and that it might be convenient to adopt some of their ideas or even enter into an alliance with them.

This approach was the basis of German National Communism, whose possibilities impressed quite a number of people in the Weimar Republic of 1919 and the early 1920s. While the Communist, Karl Radek, was interned in the Berlin prison of Moabit, he was visited among others by Baron Eugen von Reibnitz, a colleague of Marshal Ludendorff in the Cadet Corps and "the champion in officers' circles, not only of alliance with Soviet Russia, but of the so-called peaceful revolution. Reibnitz was of the opinion that the central task of restoring the productive forces of Germany was insoluble without the nationalization of industry and without factory committees." The great Walter Rathenau, himself a representative of vast industrial interests, and another visitor in what Professor E. H. Carr has called "Radek's Political Salon," admitted that there could be no return to the old capitalist order. A new society, in which capitalism, the right of inheritance, the old social categories, would disappear, in which the most intelligent and the strongest would be the leaders, should be created by the working class under the leadership of an aristocracy of intellect which would closely resemble Dr. Rathenau himself. In another vein, fifteen years later, one of France's most influential economic journalists argued that socialist opposition to liberal individualism attempts to provide the kind of collective awareness which liberal capitalism lacks, and that the only hope of neutralizing the socialist appeal lay in the production of a collective and unifying ideology that could match it. . . .

This kind of awareness, this kind of scruple, had not played a very significant role in the nineteenth-century middle-class thought—especially not after 1848. The first to discover the drawbacks of liberalism had been those well intentioned members of the middle and upper classes whose reason, conscience, or sensibilities had been shocked by the sufferings of the urban poor. Their yearnings for a better organized society would survive as one of the strands of our story. More concrete political action could be expected from those who first felt the ill effects of liberal free enterprise: that is, the propertyless workers. Particularly in the great and growing cities of Western Europe, industrialization created a class of permanent wage earners devoid of property and therefore not commited to individualistic principles. Such people were amenable to collectivistic arguments, first of a nationalistic, then of a socialistic sort. . . .

Tariffs, commercial competition, threats of war on the one hand; the growing effectiveness of syndicalist organization and its more active participation in national and international politics on the other—all emphasized the superior effectiveness of groups over unorganized individuals. Meanwhile, the middle classes were facing problems of their own. Where earlier opportunities had not been lacking for the small entrepreneur to set up in business, make money, and rise in the social scale, now big business, big capital, growing labor, taxing and interfering states, were all squeezing him out of business. And so, beginning in the late ninteenth century, certain sections of the middle classes, threatened especially by the encroachments and the competition of great capitalist enterprises, began to consider their danger and to welcome or, at least, to heed collectivistic doctrines which stressed the need to regulate the workings of capital in order to protect the people (in this occurrence themselves) from private exploitation.

First, they resented the kind of unregulated speculation that made unwitting investors lose their savings in spectacular crashes; then they came to fear the competition of large department stores, chain stores, and trusts. . . . It was no longer enough for a man to work hard, save, and thrive: a big combine could put him out of business, his savings might disappear overnight, because of obscure machinations he ignored; his farm might become useless because people halfway across the world could produce more wheat and fatter sheep and ship them to his country and still undersell him. This seemed sheer chaos to the little man, and it was easy to persuade him that the economic developments which were endangering and eliminating small and medium enterprises, and which affected farmers as well, were typical of a system that was intrinsically anarchic.

In a sense that was true. But economic anarchy had gone unnoticed as long as its possibilities had helped rather than hindered the making of money. Now, liberal economics started to look threatening to a number of people who had in the past benefited from it; and, by a natural equation, it became connected in many minds with liberal politics, similarly competitive and similarly anarchic, which had better be replaced (the argument began to be heard) by a more reliable order: restrictive, protective, controlling private enterprise in order to protect it, not to destroy it.

Naturally, most of these people did not know how to formulate their resentments and their claims, and their plight did not attract much attention from the theorists until the twenties and the thirties when it became really widespread and manifest. But this seems to be the basis of the right-wing spectrum noticeable during the last half-century, and also the basis of differences of orientation to be found within the so-called right: the difference between conservative and radical tendencies. Those who benefited from the established order were firmly conservative, and so were some of the small, threatened property owners. But the mass of the latter, together with those whom the system stripped of the security and the income which they once enjoyed, would oscillate between variants of radicalism, all of which repudiated liberalism and capitalism, some envisaging a return to a sort of Jeffersonian golden age, while others wanted to forge ahead, through revolution, to a new collectivistic social order.

Insofar as they all suspected or feared the class-covetousness of socialist claims and ignored the class character of their own resentments, these people were united in opposition to conventional socialism and communism. They were united, too, by a common belief in the national entity and in the value of national definition—a belief which the Marxists traditionally denied or, at least, played down. Nationalism was going to furnish the ideological basis on which otherwise divergent sections of the right would join in temporary alliances, and also the inspiration for doctrines of reform which the less conservative sections could accept, adopt, and follow. . . .

NATIONALISM

. . . In 1792 and 1848, nationalists were still humanistic and universalistic: Italians, Poles, or Frenchmen would not only save themselves, but they would save the world. Affirming their right to freedom, they affirmed the same right for others, too. By 1870, let alone by 1918, they had all become self-assertive to the point of aggression. The nationalist ideology, once it had been accepted, had taken up the narrow opportunism of traditional politics. In other words, where nationalism captured the state, it was in turn captured by the state; and it was used (consciously or not) to rationalize actions and policies which were not specifically nationalistic. The relations between nationalists in different countries were basically changed as soon as any of them graduated from mere theory to real state power. When they became bureaucrats and politicians, the nationalists assumed the implications and the responsibilities of economies and policies that were based not on cooperation, but on competition. Their ideology became a new flag to wave over the old-fashioned armies of opportunistic power politics.

Economic Factors. Something else happened to complicate the problems and the nature of nationalism. Just when its ideology had established itself and pervaded the public mind, nationalism had to cope with rapid changes that were taking place in the scale of economic and industrial activity. At the turn of the eighteenth to the nineteenth century, nationalism had been a practical innovation. The national state had been an improvement over the congeries of autonomous units it replaced: it offered people more scope and a wider area of action. But by the end of the nineteenth century, the needs and the pressures of a vastly more productive, more integrated, more complex economy were already finding this scope too narrow. The nation as an economic unit was being involved in a much vaster world market. A new kind of collectivism—world collectivism—pressed in upon the more limited—national—one. And nationalism had to become defensive and to resist the intrusion of new forces and new ideas—just because the expansive pressures of modern industry were making it aggressive and because the self-sufficient nation-state that had been such an advance only a little while before was becoming less viable and also more involved and more vulnerable in the cat's cradle of modern world economy.

These same expansive forces, which accentuated the doctrinal contradictions within nationalism, also generated a new doctrinal challenge outside it—socialism, which appears toward the end of the nineteenth century as the opponent and the foil of nationalism, but which is actually the product of the same assumptions that were part of nationalism itself.

In 1789, men had set out to organize their world according to their own laws and not to those of some external order. To do this, they had transferred political thought and action from the private to the collective level; the first stage of this revolution had been political. But it did not take long before claims were advanced for a further revolution, a social revolution, which would serve more than a limited minority of the middle class: a revolution of and for the whole people, which would set up a new economic and social order and not just a new form of government, which would (in other words) go further toward fulfilling the logical conclusions of the principles of 1789.

By the end of the nineteenth century these views were identified with socialism. But they could just as easily be identified with nationalism. If they were not, it is because the connection between nationalism and collectivism had in the meantime been lost from sight. And this had happened for a very practical reason: as the middle classes achieved their political objectives in some kind of national and constitutional order, and as they attained their economic objectives by gaining opportunity and prosperity and security, the old slogans of revolutionary and collectivistic self-determination did not suit them any more. These people believed in the nation, and they believed in the general will; but they also believed in property—and property was being challenged by the ideas of the socialists.

How were they going to reconcile the new reality and the old doctrine? How were they going to reconcile the collectivistic implications of what they believed with the collectivistic demands of what they withstood? How were they going to join—or openly join—the camp of established order, which they had opposed for so long? There was the problem: a middle class, which had been identified with the party of movement, achieves its objectives and begins to appreciate the *status quo*. But while its interests call for stability, its ideology remains an ideology of movement and reform. How can it become a party of order and yet continue to flatter itself that it still represents movement and progress? The way to do so was to emphasize that part of its doctrine whose dynamism did not threaten its interests. Here nationalism was useful: against the divisive doctrines of class war, the erstwhile revolutionaries (now replete) proclaimed the old Jacobin doctrine of national unity; against the subversive doctrines of socialist internationalism, they reaffirmed the reality of the nation in arms, facing a foreign foe. When they had persuaded themselves that this is what nationalism means, they were able to march into the conservative camp—the camp of property and the status quo—with a clear conscience. For a while, after the turn of the century, nationalism was going to provide the slogans of the respectable right against the collectivistic ideas of the subversive left. This was paradoxical, because nationalism had been the first to challenge property rights for the sake of a superior interest; now it was mobilized to defend property and the established order that went with it.

Conjunction of Right and Left. Under the surface, all sorts of ferments were working, both on the right and on the left. Many socialist leaders were patriotic at heart. They mouthed the slogans of international working-class unity, they called on the workers of the world to unite against their class enemies, but actually they feared the competition of foreign labor and hated the national enemy much more than the class enemy. This was best shown in 1914, when, on the outbreak of war, the workers abandoned class for national resentments and rallied like everybody else to the cause of the Fatherland.

At the same time, however, many right-wing nationalist leaders were social radicals, and they had their own ideas about what nationalism meant. The conservative right, which was glad enough to use the slogans of nationalism, was too conservative to consider the more radical implications of the doctrine. And this was going to bring about a split in the right—between nondoctrinaire conservatives on the one hand, and radical doctrinaries on the other—a split hidden from sight much of the time by the common use of nationalist slogans, but which we can now trace, in Germany and Austria and France, right back to the end of the nineteenth century.

Men like Maurice Barrès in France described themselves as National Socialists. They realized that national unity implied social justice, that national power implied the planned use of national resources, that national harmony might mean the equalization or the redistribution of wealth and opportunity and economic power. Being doctrinaire, they were willing to be ruthless. Being intellectuals, they did not feel the need to maintain the established order at all costs. Putting the nation first and property second, they found that their theories were leading them toward Jacobinism—even while the official left-wing heirs of the Jacobins were moving in the opposite direction.

These national-collectivist ideas were going to be put into practice during the First World War: planning, direction, compulsion, taxation. The nations mobilized their resources, regardless of the property rights that conservative nationalism was supposed to defend. When the war ended and the Jacobin measures were allowed to lapse, an ideological residue remained: when you are hard pressed, you can mobilize the nation. And the first to take this advice was a heretical socialist, Mussolini. . . .

CONCLUSION

Reaction. Twentieth-century fascism is a by-product of disintegrating liberal democracy. Loss of hope in the possibilities of existing order and society, disgust with their corruption and ineffectiveness, above all the society's evident loss of confidence in itself, all these produce or spur a revolutionary mood in which the only issue lies in catastrophic action—but always with a strong social tinge: "I place my only hope in the continuation of socialist progress through fascisms," writes Drieu. And the editor of the French fascist publication, the *Insurgent*, Jean-Pierre Maxence, would call insurgents of all parties to join "the front of united youth, for bread, for grandeur and for liberty, in immense disgust with capitalist democracy." From this angle, as from many others, fascism looks much like the Jacobinism of our time.

There is no doubt that, at least in France, it was the failure, real or apparent, of the established order to stand up for itself and for its own —it was this failure that created and recruited the troops of a certain fascist reaction. But the appearance of such movements may also be cited in evidence of the middle classes' determination to defend themselves—a mood which a Paris candidate expressed when she told her electors that she "remained violently moderate."

Movements of this sort can often be the pure expression of reaction. A social class or a body of men think their interests are threatened and organize to defend them. There is nothing "social" about such a reaction, it is hardly even a pretense. And since both reactionaries and fascists exalt violence as part of their policy, the contradiction between the former, who want settled order and security, and the latter, who want to destroy the settled order, is lost from sight. But, while social reaction and social thoughtlessness have made their contribution to fascism, we have seen that fascist doctrines and the fascist temper are far from reactionary in themselves.

Characteristics. The confusion is understandable. For though fascist movements are revolutionary, they can only triumph in a situation which brings grist to their mill, by displacing people and resources from the camp of order into a no man's land where they will listen to their appeals. There is, indeed, a profound connection between this revolutionary character and what we know of fascism's appeal to youth. In one sense, we recognize in all fascist-type movements a rising of younger generations against the old who keep them from the manger. In 1933, Blum and Herriot in France were 61, Baldwin was 66, Ramsay Macdonald and the Belgian Socialist leader Emile Vandervelde 67, Hindenburg 86. Hitler and Mussolini were 44, Mosley 37, Doriot 35, Codreanu 31, José Antonio 30, Degrelle 24. Figures like these speak for themselves.

In a profounder sense, however, a revolutionary movement must recruit people who are all free in social position or in spirit. One cannot take great risks, run the chance of scandal or arrest, be available for anything at all hours, if the thought of career or mortgage or an income holds one back. Only the very poor, the very young (also perhaps the very rich, but there are few of those and even fewer who want to change the order from which they benefit), can qualify for revolutionary action, as opposed to writing or to talk; and they envisage it quite often as a way of ceasing to be nonentities or to be poor. The danger that the activist flame may be stifled by public position or material concerns is one all revolutionary parties face; and they resolve it by elitism, and by decreeing that the gains of any victory shall be not particular but collective. They follow up their idealistic appeal with the attempt to connect private success with that of the collective and to keep the militant from acquiring such vested interests in the status quo as to lose interest in continued revolution. Then, as and when they can, they do their best to train the youth to transfer its self-interest from self to party, that is to the nation.

Meanwhile, like all minority movements, the fascists can only succeed when social circumstances provide a public their appeal attracts or, at least, the resources that will help them win it. This was what happened to the *fascios*, to the Nazis and, briefly, to the French leagues of the middle twenties. In France, however, as in Britain and Belgium, conditions never became bad enough for a tide of sympathy to float the local movements into power. Fascist and National Socialist movements were fated to remain minoritarian and (while their doctrine often incorporated measures we should call progressive) to win only by violence or to disappear. Alternately, a fascist movement whose revolutionary and "social" character made it popular enough to attain power by legal means might be suppressed, as in Romania, by conservative forces, suspected and kept at arm's length as in Hungary, or used and then crushed as in Spain. In any case, the identification between fascism and reaction is widely off the mark.

The identification of fascism and National Socialism is more understandable and better justified. It should be possible, however, to distinguish between the two, even if only at the doctrinal level. For, while what people say about their ideas does not always match what they actually do, it does reflect their assumptions, and it is usually respected—if only in the breach.

Fascism. Fascism . . . rejects theory in favor of practice and relies largely on the attraction of that "fever" to which I have referred. The fascist ethos is emotional and sentimental: at that level the ends of action count less than action itself, and the forces that lead men into the fascist camp can be enlisted on any side whatever, provided they are given an opportunity to indulge themselves—the more violent, the better. This indiscriminate nature of fascism appears in figures as far apart as Mussolini, Doriot, and Degrelle, who militated in turn in a number of parties, pursuing action rather than ideas, power rather than principles.

National Socialism. The National Socialist, on the other hand, seems much more theoretical. He may use theory merely to rationalize, but he respects it. Whatever he may pretend, words and ideas count for him as much as actions, and sometimes they replace them. What men like Déat seem to have sought was a new *system* which, unlike old ones that had been tried and found wanting, would help rebuild or repair the failing structure of the state.

Although the program of the Arrow Cross or of the Iron Guard was profoundly mystical, the spirit animating such movements was of a different order from that which we find in the *fascios* or in Rex. A doctrine may be crackpot though dogmatic: the theories of Rosenberg, of Szalasi, of Quisling, were both; but they differ less among themselves than they do from the cheerful pragmatism of Mussolini or Degrelle.

All this may mean that the ideological National Socialist (the kind we may, for instance, find in France) will content himself with theorizing, but never go beyond the grandiose plans and dire threats he lavishes in print. It also lays him open to the charge (as brought against the Nazis) of using his theories as bait for the unwary, while in practice he advances through deals with the forces of capital, which are perhaps using him after all, as John Strachey suggested. It is quite obvious, however, that the Nazis of all people were ready to make the most extraordinary sacrifices for the sake of their theories and their twisted ideals.

It is true that Hitler was an opportunist who declared his aims very clearly and very early in the game, and then temporized on their accomplishment. But the deals and the sacrifices that he made, first to get into power and then to affirm his power, were expedients he abandoned as soon as possible. Industrialists like Fritz Thyssen, conservatives like Franz von Papen, moderate economists like Schacht, moderate diplomats like Neurath were shed, or brought to heel, or crushed, as and when circumstances permitted; likewise the army. True, about 1927 and again in 1934, Hitler toned down the radical aspect of his movement in order to win the support of conservative forces that he had to conciliate. But in the next decade the Nazi state affirmed its control ever more totally over every sector of national life and, had it won the war, there would have been little that escaped its direction, little that remained private except in name.

Differences. This, then, is where the basic difference seems to lie: fascism is pragmatically activist, National Socialism theoretically motivated or, at least, expressed. Both aim to conquer power and that center of power which is the modern state. But in one case the power will be wielded pragmatically and piecemeal, simply for its own sake, while the party which has been its instrument may gradually be abandoned. In the other, power will be used to realize an anterior plan or a series of plans inspired by the original doctrine; and then the party may become a Church—a Church and a dynamo.

Therein lie the nature and the major characteristics of movements which between them encompass a vast area of contemporary experience. Conceived in Europe, like nationalism and Marxism, fascism and National Socialism have become articles for export. The circumstances in which they grew, the sentiments that inspired them, the characteristics we have noted, may be found with variations in most political situations of the world today. Neither sympathy nor dislike are by themselves a satisfactory reaction to attitudes and ideas with which we must learn to cope. Fascist movements demand further investigation if we are to understand the many problems which confront us here and now.

Seymour Lipset

FASCISM AS THE EXTREMISM
OF THE CENTER

*Seymour Martin Lipset (b. New York, 1922) was educated in sociology at City
College in New York and Columbia University. He is a prolific writer on a
variety of subjects within the social sciences and is especially concerned with the
problems of class, status, and social mobility in industrial societies. He is presently Professor of Government and Social Relations at Harvard University.*

. . . Much of the discussion between Marxist and non-Marxist scholars
before 1945 was devoted to an analysis of fascism in power and focused
on whether the Nazis or other fascist parties were actually strengthening
the economic institutions of capitalism or creating a new postcapitalist
social order similar to Soviet bureaucratic totalitarianism.

While an anlaysis of the actual behavior of parties in office is crucial
to an understanding of their functional significance, the social base and
ideology of any movement must also be analyzed if it is to be truly understood. A study of the social bases of different modern mass movements suggests that each major social stratum has both democratic and
extremist political expressions. The extremist movements of the left,
right, and center (communism and Peronism, traditional authoritarianism, and fascism) are based primarily on the working, upper, and middle
classes, respectively. The term "fascism" has been applied at one time or
another to all of these varieties of extremism, but an analytical ex-
amination of the social base and ideology of each reveals their different
characters.

From Seymour Martin Lipset, Political Man *(Garden City, N.Y.: 1960), pp.
127–37, 176–79. Copyright 1959, 1960 by Seymour Martin Lipset. Reprinted by
permission of the author and Doubleday & Company, Inc.*

The political and sociological analysis of modern society in terms of left, center, and right goes back to the days of the first French Republic when the delegates were seated, according to their political coloration, in a continuous semicircle from the most radical and egalitarian on the left to the most moderate and aristocratic on the right. The identification of the left with advocacy of social reform and egalitarianism; the right, with aristocracy and conservatism, deepened as politics became defined as the clash between classes. Nineteenth-century conservatives and Marxists alike joined in the assumption that the socioeconomic cleavage is the most basic in modern society. Since democracy has become institutionalized and the conservatives' fears that universal suffrage would mean the end of private property have declined, many people have begun to argue that the analysis of politics in terms of left and right and class conflict oversimplifies and distorts reality. However, the tradition of political discourse, as well as political reality, has forced most scholars to retain these basic concepts, although other dimensions, like religious differences or regional conflicts, account for political behavior which does not follow class lines.[1]

Before 1917 extremist political movements were usually thought of as a rightist phenomenon. Those who would eliminate democracy generally sought to restore monarchy or the rule of the aristocrats. After 1917 politicians and scholars alike began to refer to both left and right extremism, i.e., communism and fascism. In this view, extremists at either end of the political continuum develop into advocates of dictatorship, while the moderates of the center remain the defenders of democracy. This chapter will attempt to show that this is an error—that extremist ideologies and groups can be classified and analyzed in the same terms as democratic groups, i.e., right, left, and *center*. The three positions resemble their democratic parallels in both the compositions of their social bases and the contents of their appeals. While comparisons of all three positions on the democratic and extremist continuum are of intrinsic interest, this chapter concentrates on the politics of the center, the most neglected type of political extremism, and that form of "left" extremism sometimes called "fascism"—Peronism—as manifested in Argentina and Brazil.

The center position among the democratic tendencies is usually called liberalism. In Europe where it is represented by various parties like the

---

[1] In spite of the complexities of French politics, the foremost students of elections in that country find that they must classify parties and alternatives along the left-right dimension. See F. Goguel. *Géographie des élections françaises de 1870 à 1951, Cahiers de la fondation nationale des sciences politiques*, No. 27 (Paris: Librairie Armand Colin, 1951).

French Radicals, the Dutch and Belgian Liberals, and others, the liberal position means: in economics—a commitment to laissez-faire ideology, a belief in the vitality of small business, and opposition to strong trade unions; in politics—a demand for minimal government intervention and regulation; in social ideology—support of equal opportunity for achievement, opposition to aristocracy, and opposition to enforced equality of income; in culture—anticlericalism and antitraditionalism.

If we look at the supporters of the three major positions in most democratic countries, we find a fairly logical relationship between ideology and social base. The socialist left derives its strength from manual workers and the poorer rural strata; the conservative right is backed by the rather well-to-do elements—owners of large industry and farms, the managerial and free professional strata—and those segments of the less privileged groups who have remained involved in traditionalist institutions, particularly the Church. The democratic center is backed by the middle classes, especially small businessmen, white-collar workers, and the anticlerical sections of the professional classes.

The different extremist groups have ideologies which correspond to those of their democratic counterparts. The classic fascist movements have represented the extremism of the center. Fascist ideology, though antiliberal in its glorification of the state, has been similar to liberalism in its opposition to big business, trade unions, and the socialist state. It has also resembled liberalism in its distaste for religion and other forms of traditionalism. And, as we shall see later, the social characteristics of Nazi voters in pre-Hitler Germany and Austria resembled those of the liberals much more than they did those of the conservatives.

The largest group of left extremists are the communists. . . . The communists are clearly revolutionary, opposed to the dominant strata, and based on the lower classes. There is, however, another form of left extremism which, like right extremism, is often classified under the heading of fascism. This form, Peronism, largely found in poorer underdeveloped countries, appeals to the lower strata against the middle and upper classes. It differs from communism in being nationalistic, and has usually been the creation of nationalist army officers seeking to create a more vital society by destroying the corrupt privileged strata which they believe have kept the masses in poverty, the economy underdeveloped, and the army demoralized and underpaid.

Conservative or rightist extremist movements have arisen at different periods in modern history, ranging from the Horthyites in Hungary, the Christian Social party of Dollfuss in Austria, the Stahlhelm and other nationalists in pre-Hitler Germany, and Salazar in Portugal, to the pre-1958 Gaullist movements and the monarchists in contemporary France and Italy. The right extremists are conservative, not revolutionary. They seek to change political institutions in order to preserve or restore cultural and economic ones, while extremists of the center and left seek to use political means for cultural and social revolution. The ideal of the right extremist is not a totalitarian ruler, but a monarch, or a traditionalist who acts like one. Many such movements—in Spain, Austria, Hungary, Germany, and Italy—have been explicitly monarchist, and De Gaulle returned monarchical rights and privileges to the French presidency. Not surprisingly, the supporters of these movements differ from those of the centrists; they tend to be wealthier, and—more important in terms of mass support—more religious.

"FASCISM" AND THE MIDDLE CLASS

The thesis that fascism is basically a middle-class movement representing a protest against both capitalism *and* socialism, big business *and* big unions, is far from original. Many analysts have suggested it ever since fascism and Nazism first appeared on the scene. Nearly twenty-five years ago, the economist David Saposs stated it well:

Fascism . . . [is] the extreme expression of middle-classism or populism. . . . The basic ideology of the middle class is populism.
Their ideal was an independent small property-owning class consisting of merchants, mechanics, and farmers. This element . . . now designated as middle class, sponsored a system of private property, profit, and competition on an entirely different basis from that conceived by capitalism. . . . From its very inception it opposed "big business" or what has now become known as capitalism.
Since the war the death knell of liberalism and individualism has been vociferously, albeit justly sounded. But since liberalism and individualism are of middle-class origin, it has been taken for granted that this class has also been eliminated as an effective social force. As a matter of fact, populism is now as formidable a force as it has ever been. And the middle class is more vigorously assertive than ever. . . .[2]

[2] David J. Saposs, "The Role of the Middle Class in Social Development: Fascism, Populism, Communism, Socialism," in *Economic Essays in Honor of Wesley Clair Mitchell* (New York: Columbia University Press, 1935), pp. 395, 397, 400. An even earlier analysis by André Siegfried, based on a detailed ecological study of voting patterns in part of France from 1871 to 1912, suggested that the petty bourgeoisie who had been considered the classic source of French democratic ideology were becoming the principal recruiting grounds for extremist movements. Siegfried pointed out that though they are "by nature egalitarian, democratic, and envious . . . they

And although some have attributed the lower middle-class support for Nazism to the specific economic difficulties of the 1930s, the political scientist, Harold Lasswell, writing in the depths of the depression, suggested that middle-class extremism flowed from trends inherent in capitalist industrial society which would continue to affect the middle class even if its economic position improved.

Insofar as Hitlerism is a desperation reaction of the lower middle classes, it continues a movement which began during the closing years of the nineteenth century. Materially speaking, it is not necessary to assume that the small shopkeepers, teachers, preachers, lawyers, doctors, farmers, and craftsmen were worse off at the end than they had been in the middle of the century. Psychologically speaking, however, the lower middle class was increasingly overshadowed by the workers and the upper bourgeoisie, whose unions, cartels, and parties took the center of the stage. The psychological impoverishment of the lower middle class precipitated emotional insecurities within the personalities of its members, thus fertilizing the ground for the various movements of mass protest through which the middle classes might revenge themselves.[3]

As the relative position of the middle class declined and its resentments against on-going social and economic trends continued, its "liberal" ideology—the support of individual rights against large-scale power—changed from that of a revolutionary class to that of a reactionary class. Once liberal doctrines had supported the bourgeoisie in their fight against the remnants of the feudal and monarchical order, and against the limitations demanded by mercantilist rulers and the Church. A liberal ideology opposed to Throne and Altar and favoring a limited state emerged. This ideology was not only revolutionary in political terms; it fulfilled some of the functional requirements for efficient industrialization. As Max Weber pointed out, the development of the capi-

---

are fearful above all of new economic conditions which threatened to eliminate them, crushed between the aggressive capitalism of the great companies and the increasing rise of the working people. They place great hopes in the Republic, and they do not cease being republican or egalitarian. But they are in that state of discontent, from which the Boulangisms marshal their forces, in which reactionary demagogues see the best ground in which to agitate, and in which is born passionate resistance to certain democratic reforms." André Siegfried. *Tableau politique de la France de l'ouest sous la troisième république* (Paris: Librairie Armand Colin, 1913), p. 413.

[3] Harold Lasswell, "The Psychology of Hitlerism," *The Political Quarterly*, IV (1933), p. 374.

talist system (which in his analysis coincides with industrialization) necessitated the abolition of artificial internal boundaries, the creation of an open international market, the establishment of law and order, and relative international peace.[4]

But the aspirations and ideology which underlay eighteenth- and nineteenth-century liberalism and populism have a different meaning and serve a different function in the advanced industrial societies of the twentieth century. Resisting largescale organizations and the growth of state authority challenges some of the fundamental characteristics of our present society, since large industry and a strong and legitimate labor movement are necessary for a stable, modernized social structure, and government regulation and heavy taxes seem an inevitable concomitant. To be against business bureaucracies, trade unions, and state regulation is both unrealistic and to some degree irrational. As Talcott Parsons has put it, the "new negative orientation to certain primary aspects of the maturing modern social order has above all centered in the symbol of 'capitalism'. . . . The reaction against the 'ideology' of the rationalization of society is the principal aspect at least of the ideology of fascism." [5]

While continuing conflict between management and labor is an integral part of large-scale industrialism, the small businessman's desire to retain an important place for himself and his social values is "reactionary"—not in the Marxist sense of slowing down the wheels of revolution, but from the perspective of the inherent trends of a modern industrial society. Sometimes the efforts of the small business stratum to resist or reverse the process take the form of democratic liberal movements, like the British Liberal party, the French Radicals, or the American Taft Republicans. Such movements have failed to stop the trends which their adherents oppose, and as another sociologist, Martin Trow, recently noted: "The tendencies which small businessmen fear—of concentration and centralization—proceed without interruption in depression, war and prosperity, and irrespective of what party is in power; thus

---

[4] See also Karl Polanyi, *The Great Transformation* (New York: Farrar and Rinehart, 1944).

[5] Talcott Parsons, "Some Sociological Aspects of the Fascist Movement," in his *Essays in Sociological Theory* (Glencoe: The Free Press, 1954), pp. 133–34. Marx himself pointed out that "the small manufacturer, the small merchant, the artisan, the peasant, all fight against the [big] bourgeois, in order to protect their position as a middle class from being destroyed. They are, however, not revolutionary, but conservative. Even more, they are reactionary, they look for a way to reverse the path of history," quoted in S. S. Nilson, "Wahlsoziologische Probleme des Nationalsozialismus," *Zeitschrift für die Gesamte Staatswissenschaft*, CX (1954), p. 295.

they are *always* disaffected. . . ." [6] It is not surprising, therefore, that under certain conditions small businessmen turn to extremist political movements, either fascism or antiparliamentary populism, which in one way or another express contempt for parliamentary democracy. These movements answer some of the same needs as the more conventional liberal parties; they are an outlet for the stratification strains of the middle class in a mature industrial order. But while liberalism attempts to cope with the problems by legitimate social changes and "reforms" ("reforms" which would, to be sure, reverse the modernization process), fascism and populism propose to solve the problems by taking over the state and running it in a way which will restore the old middle classes' economic security and high standing in society, and at the same time reduce the power and status of big capital and big labor.

The appeal of extremist movements may also be a response by different strata of the population to the social effects of industrialization at different stages of its development. These variations are set in sharp relief by a comparison of the organized threats to the democratic process in societies at various stages of industrialization. As I have already shown, working-class extremism, whether communist, anarchist, revolutionary socialist, or Peronist, is most commonly found in societies undergoing rapid industrialization, or in those where the process of industrialization did not result in a predominantly industrial society, like the Latin countries of southern Europe. Middle-class extremism occurs in countries characterized by both large-scale capitalism and a powerful labor movement. Right-wing extremism is most common in less developed economies, in which the traditional conservative forces linked to throne and altar remain strong. Since some countries, like France, Italy, or Weimar Germany, have possessed strata in all three sets of circumstances, all three types of extremist politics sometimes exist in the same country. Only the well-to-do, highly industrialized and urbanized nations seem immune to the virus, but even in the United States and Canada there is evidence that the self-employed are somewhat disaffected.

The different political reactions of similar strata at different points in the industrialization process are clearly delineated by a comparison of the politics of certain Latin American countries with those of Western Europe. The more well-to-do Latin American countries today resemble Europe in the nineteenth century; they are experiencing industrial growth while their working classes are still relatively unorganized into trade unions and political parties, and reservoirs of traditional con-

---

[6] Martin A. Trow, "Small Businessmen, Political Tolerance, and Support for McCarthy," *American Journal of Sociology*, LXIV (1958), pp. 279–80.

servatism still exist in their rural populations. The growing middle class in these countries, like its nineteenth-century European counterpart, supports a democratic society by attempting to reduce the influence of the anticapitalist traditionalists and the arbitrary power of the military.[7] To the extent that there is a social base at this stage of economic development for extremist politics, it lies not in the middle classes but in the growing, still unorganized working classes who are suffering from the tensions inherent in rapid industrialization. These workers have provided the primary base of support for the only large-scale "fascist" movements in Latin America—those of Peron in the Argentine and Vargas in Brazil. These movements, like the communist ones with which they have sometimes been allied, appeal to the "displaced masses" of newly industrializing countries.

The real question to answer is: which strata are most "displaced" in each country? In some, it is the new working class, or the working class which was never integrated in the total society, economically or politically; in others, it is the small businessmen and other relatively independent entrepreneurs (small farm owners, provincial lawyers) who feel oppressed by the growing power and status of unionized workers and by large-scale corporative and governmental bureaucracies. In still others, it is the conservative and traditionalist elements who seek to preserve the old society from the values of socialism and liberalism. Fascist ideology in Italy, for example, arose out of an opportunistic movement which sought at various times to appeal to all three groups, and remained sufficiently amorphous to permit appeals to widely different strata, depending on national variations as to who were most "displaced." [8] Since

[7] For an analysis of the political role of the rapidly growing Latin-American middle classes see John J. Johnson, *Political Change in Latin America—the Emergence of the Middle Sectors* (Stanford: Stanford University Press, 1958). The different political propensities of a social group at successive stages of industrialization are indicated by James Bryce's comment in 1912 that "the absence of that class of small landowners which is the soundest and most stable element in the United States and in Switzerland and is equally stable, if less politically trained, in France and parts of Germany, is a grave misfortune for South and Central America." This may have been true in an early period, before the impact of large-scale organization of the farms meant economic competition for small farmers and added them to the rank of the potential supporters of fascism, as the data on Germany and other countries discussed here show. See James Bryce, *South America· Observations and Impressions* (New York: Macmillan, 1912), p. 533.

[8] A comparison of the European middle class and the Argentine working class, which argues that each is most "displaced" in its respective environment, is contained in Gino Germani, *Integracion politica de las masas y la totalitarismo* (Buenos Aires: Colegio Libre de Estudios Superiores, 1956). See also his *Estructura social de la Argentina* (Buenos Aires: Raigal, 1955).

fascist politicians have been extremely opportunistic in their efforts to secure support, such movements have often encompassed groups with conflicting interests and values, even when they primarily expressed the needs of one stratum. Hitler, a centrist extremist, won backing from conservatives who hoped to use the Nazis against the Marxist left. And conservative extremists like Franco have often been able to retain centrists among their followers without giving them control of the movement. . . .

THE SOCIAL BASES OF FASCISM

The analysis of modern totalitarian movements has reflected the old concepts of left, right, and center. Politicians and scholars alike have seen these movements as representing the extremes of the political spectrum, hence they speak of communism as the extreme left and fascism as the extreme right. But antidemocratic ideologies as well as antidemocratic groups can be more fruitfully classified and analyzed if it is recognized that "left," "right," and "center" refer to ideologies, each of which has a moderate and an extremist version, the one parliamentary and the other extraparliamentary in its orientation. It is also necessary to recognize that a left extremist movement that is working-class based and oriented also may be militaristic, nationalistic, and anti-Marxist.[9]

While all the varieties of antidemocratic mass movements are of equal interest, I have tried here to establish the usefulness of the tripartite distinction by examining the social bases of different political movements. Data from a number of countries demonstrate that classic fascism is a movement of the propertied middle classes, who for the most part normally support liberalism, and that it is opposed by the conservative strata, who have, however, at different times backed conservative antiparliamentary regimes. The conservative regimes are, in contrast to centrist ones, nonrevolutionary and nontotalitarian. In a conservative dictatorship, one is not expected to give total loyalty to the regime, to

[9] Some have found it difficult to accept the fact that a leader and movement whose ideology, symbolism, and methods resembled Fascism and Nazism could in fact not be rightist. Thus a book written before Peron consolidated his power suggested that he represented the interests of the *estancieros*, the large landlords who had controlled the Conservative party and ruled the Argentine for much of its history. See Felix J. Weil, *Argentine Riddle* (New York: John Day, 1944). Even *Time* magazine wrote in 1951 "as though it were not news to anybody, that 'Peron operates a state essentially modeled on the classic Nazi-Fascist pattern.'" *Time*, May 21, 1951, p. 43, cited in George I. Blankstein, *Peron's Argentina* (Chicago: University of Chicago Press, 1953), p. 277.

join a party or other institutions, but simply to keep out of politics. Though the dictatorship of the Austrian clerical conservatives has been described as fascist, the differences between it and its Nazi successor are abundantly clear. Similarly, although Franco is backed by the Spanish fascists—the Falange—his regime has been dominated by conservative authoritarians. The party has never been allowed to dominate the society; most institutions remain independent of the state and the party, and the opposition is not asked to conform or join, only to abstain from organized opposition.

Although a distinction may be made among these movements analytically, in any given country there is considerable overlap, as in the case of the Spanish Nationalists. Basically revolutionary movements like Nazism did secure some support from conservatives who agreed with its nationalistic and anti-Marxist aspects. Italian fascism represented a coalition of both centrist and conservative extremism led by a pure opportunist. It would be a mistake, however, to conclude from the absence of movements which are purely one or the other variety that the analytic distinction is of merely speculative interest. Recent political movements—Poujadism, McCarthyism, Gaullism—all exhibit particular characteristics associated with the nature of their social base. If we want to preserve and extend parliamentary democracy, we must understand the source of threats to it, and threats from conservatives are as different from those originating in the middle-class center as these are from communism.

Extremist movements have much in common. They appeal to the disgruntled and the psychologically homeless, to the personal failures, the socially isolated, the economically insecure, the uneducated, unsophisticated, and authoritarian persons at every level of the society. As Heberle puts it, such movements are supported by "those who for some reason or other had failed to make a success in their business or occupation, and those who had lost their social status or were in danger of losing it. . . . The masses of the organized [Nazi] party members consisted therefore before 1933 largely of people who were outsiders in their own class, black sheep in their family, thwarted in their ambitions. . . ." [10] As far back as the 1890s, Engels described those who "throng to the working-class parties in all countries" as "those who have nothing to look forward to from the official world or have come to the end of their tether with it—opponents of inoculation, supporters of abstemious-

---

[10] R. Heberle, *From Democracy to Nazism* (Baton Rouge: Louisiana State University Press, 1945), p. 10.

ness, vegetarians, antivivisectionists, nature-healers, free-community preachers whose communities have fallen to pieces, authors of new theories on the origin of the universe, unsuccessful or unfortunate inventors, victims of real or imaginary injustice . . . honest fools and dishonest swindlers." [11] It is often men from precisely such origins who give the fanatical and extremist character to these movements and form the core of believers.[12] But the various extremist movements, like their democratic alternatives, wax or wane depending on whether they can win and retain the support of the strata whom they are trying to represent and lead.

[11] Friedrich Engels, "On the History of Early Christianity," in K. Marx and F. Engels, *On Religion* (Moscow: Foreign Languages Publishing House, 1957), p. 319.

[12] See G. Almond, *The Appeals of Communism* (Princeton: Princeton University Press, 1954), Chaps. 9 and 10, esp. pp. 258–61.

John Weiss

FASCISM AS THE EXTREMISM
OF THE RIGHT

John Weiss (b. Detroit, Michigan, 1927) graduated from Columbia University
in 1958. Especially interested in intellectual history, he is the author of a book
on the German socialist thinker Moses Hess. The selections presented here are
from Weiss's volume in a series on major traditions of world civilization. Weiss
is Professor of History at Lehman College in New York.

. . . The original and contemporaneous nature of fascism has been, I
think, much overemphasized. Certainly there has been no fascist tradition if by that one means a continuous and long-term fascistic response
to social change by powerful and established groups. Mussolini's words,
"I am a reactionary and a revolutionary," are appropriate here. Fascism,
after all, is a conservative social movement, however radical. As such, it
is closely related to ideas, interests, and classes active in Western civilization since the first great challenge to conservative values during the
French Revolution of 1789. It is this relationship that has not been fully
explored. It is fortunate, however, that few attempt any longer to explain
the origins of fascism and national socialism by reference to the supposed unique and collective guilt of the German people, or the alleged
demonic irrationalism of modern man, or the gangsterism of a handful
of nihilistic leaders committed to power and power alone. But as yet not
enough has been done to show how the radical right plays on the fears
and represents the hopes of traditional conservatives. As I hope to show,
the reactionary revolutionaries who seized power in Italy and Germany

did so largely because they gained power and support from older conservative classes, and prestige from a previously established conservative intellectual tradition. . . .

And this is my major point: The radical right thrives in societies where older but still powerful conservative classes are threatened by rapid and modernizing social change; change which creates or gives strength to liberal and radical classes and groups antagonistic toward "the old ways." Thus, in the twentieth century, the minority of revolutionary conservatives always present in modern Europe became the needed counterreaction and the defenders of conservatism *in extremus.* Any study of fascism which centers too narrowly on the fascists and Nazis alone may miss the true significance of right-wing extremism. For without necessarily becoming party members or accepting the entire range of party principles themselves, aristocratic landlords, army officers, government and civil service officials, and important industrialists in Italy and Germany helped bring fascists and Nazis to power. In doing so, after the end of World War I, they were motivated by the fear that loss of their power, prestige, wealth, and values would shortly follow the new participation of the masses in full-fledged parliamentary democracy. The radical right was to constitute the last line of defense against the mounting liberal and radical agitation for land reform, social welfare measures, demilitarization, higher wages, and the socialization of the means of production. War, inflation, and the Great Depression certainly polarized social attitudes into extremes of left and right and opened vast opportunities to the radical right; but the basic social conflict was as old as the rise of liberalism.

Too often scholars have stressed the ideological and political differences between old conservatives and new ultraconservatives but have failed to perceive how willing the respectable conservatives have been to trade these differences with their own ultraright wing in order to prevent the victory of liberalism and radicalism and the triumph of mass democracy. The well-known slogan so often heard among the French aristocrats and businessmen in 1935 tells the story: "Better Hitler than Leon Blum." And Blum, be it noted, though ostensibly a Socialist, threatened in fact only a French version of the "New Deal." Many of the most important European industrialists shared this attitude, of course; yet the familiar Marxist formula must be discarded. Fascism was not the "last gasp of monopoly capitalism." If anything, it was the last gasp of conservatism.

Other reasons have convinced many able scholars, however, that fascism is not primarily a conservative movement. As they point out, fascists and Nazis received massive electoral support from large sections of what are normally held to be the middle and lower-middle classes: self-employed small businessmen, artisans, shopkeepers, clerical white-collar workers, lower civil servants, peasants, impoverished gentry, domestics, and pensioners. It should be remembered, however, that in general such supporters of fascism insofar as they were liberal, were so only in the sense, say, that members of the John Birch Society are liberal; i.e., they stood for the values of early nineteenth-century liberalism. Such ossified liberalism is starkly conservative in our time. It opposes representative democracy, trade-unionism, and the social legislation of the modern neoliberal welfare state; and it supports a rigid defense of the rights of private property regardless of social cost. Often caught between the competitive drive of big business and the organizing drive of trade union radicalism, these middle- and lower-middle-class groups were made desperate by the traumatic experiences of war, inflation, and depression, as well as by the overwhelming status anxieties which followed. And they felt even more threatened than the traditional conservatives by the steady advance and future prospects of welfare state liberalism and working class agitation. To both upper- and middle-class conservatives, Mussolini and Hitler offered, through street violence and totalitarian controls, the surest means of halting both international "Jewish" liberalism and trade union "bolshevism."

German and Italian experience seems to suggest that, although fascistic movements are to be found in all modern countries, fascism does not thrive unless brought to power, directly or indirectly, by a supportive alliance of preliberal power elites (semifeudal or aristocratic), reactionary industrialists, and elements of the socially frustrated lower-middle class. Such an alliance, given the acute social conflicts generated by total war and economic chaos, easily if not deliberately falls victim to the most violent enemies of liberalism and radicalism—the extremists on the right.

Once in power, however, fascists and Nazis were unwilling to act as simple lackeys of those interests which brought them to office. Indeed, they could not do so. Fascism cannot remain in control if it acts like previous despotisms or mere conservative coalition governments—governments such as those of a Franco, a Pilsudski, or a Horthy. Fascism is not traditional but revolutionary conservatism; and fascists must inaugurate unique, sweeping, and dynamic policies of systematic terror and total control over all areas of national life. For they come to power in societies where the developing historical forces of liberalism and radicalism have generated a mortal challenge to upper- and lower-class conservatives. Only where modernism (with all that that implies) has gained few social footholds, can traditional autocrats control liberalism and leftism with relative ease. The casual, sporadic, and noninstitutionalized violence of the old-fashioned despot can prevail only in an "underdeveloped" society where the liberal thrust is enfeebled by the continued existence of preliberal elites and social structures, as in Spain and Hungary. In such societies, traditional conservatives themselves may very well reject as dangerous and unnecessary the dynamic fascist totalitarian institutionalization of terror and social controls.

It is not yet understood why fascists and Nazis followed an extremist and unprecedented policy of aggressive imperialism. Traditional despotisms have usually been militarist and, when powerful, expansive. But the radical right in power conquered and exploited subject peoples with a nightmarish ruthlessness that indicates a qualitative difference. As I have sought to indicate in the following pages, the conquest and total exploitation of subject peoples was, for Nazis and fascists, an utter necessity. Otherwise, they were likely to fall victim to the very social dislocations which brought them to power, and to the internal tensions created by their totalitarian rule. When Hitler and Mussolini militarized the culture, economy, and outlook of their people, they were expressing a general tendency of the radical right everywhere to substitute military aggression and internal force for those progressive social reforms which could only strengthen the hands of their liberal and radical opponents. Since the mid-nineteenth century, militant nationalism had been the policy of conservative politics. But here too, the revolutionary reactionaries carried conservative policies to qualitatively new extremes. Even anti-Semitism, so predominant among Central and Eastern European fascists, was not simply arbitrary "scapegoatism" but an attempt to purge the nation of just those groups which, especially in Central and Eastern Europe, represented outstandingly liberal professions and radical views. In short, both terror at home and terror abroad, under fascism, were attempts to resolve political, economic, and social problems without the sacrifice of conservative and reactionary values. . . .

Fascists and National Socialists push many traditional conservative ideas to radical and vulgar extremes, but they do not abandon them. As "new" conservatives they do not want to be taken for mere defenders of the old reactionary elite, and insist endlessly that their movement is dynamic, unique, and, above all, modern. Those who write the history of social movements must be careful, however, not to take ideological statements at face value. "New" conservatives must disguise the ancient lineage of their ideas if only because a social movement that defends established interests within a mass democracy must generate a mass appeal. Because of this, most of the current generalizations about the ideology of the radical right are misleading. We are told, for example, that fascists have no program, that they are nihilistic opportunists who select from the body of their self-contradictory ideas just those which will clear the immediate obstacles on the road to power. . . . As for fascism's alleged "irrationality," it is, in reality, not so much a revolt against reason as a revolt against liberalism which liberals have found unreasonable. Like it or not, fascist ideology is international in scope, fairly self-consistent, and presents a rational, i.e., workable, if frightening. set of political, social, and economic alternatives to the reigning liberalism of the West. . . .

II

The search for a narrow and exclusive definition of fascism has been pressed too hard. As a variety of right-wing extremism, fascism must always adapt itself to the unique conservative traditions and values of the particular society it hopes to dominate. Each nation, as it were, generates the fascism it deserves. Hence, it is imperative that fascism be studied on an international scale. The reader will know from what has preceded of my own serious doubts as to the prospects for the radical right in liberalized-consensus societies. Nevertheless, this *may* be basically a question of the magnitude and nature of the social crises involved. . . .

My own judgment and knowledge, however, lead me to suspect that the greatest potential for fascism lies not in the liberal West, but rather in the dialectical polarities even now increasing in non-Western or underdeveloped societies. . . . Europe is not the only society in which liberalism and radicalism have confronted powerful remnants of feudalism and upper-class reaction in the rapid drive toward modernization and industrialism. . . .

FASCISM AS A REVOLT AGAINST MODERNISM

Barrington Moore

FASCISM AS THE HERITAGE OF CONSERVATIVE MODERNIZATION

Barrington Moore Jr. (b. 1913) is an American scholar trained in the social sciences and Russian affairs at Yale University. He is the author of a number of important studies on Soviet politics. His writings are particularly concerned with the role of ideas in social change and combine an imaginative interdisciplinary approach with a closely reasoned method of argument. At present he is senior research fellow at the Russian Research Center, Harvard University.

The second main route to the world of modern industry we have called the capitalist and reactionary one, exemplified most clearly by Germany and Japan. There capitalism took hold quite firmly in both agriculture and industry and turned them into industrial countries. But it did so without a popular revolutionary upheaval. What tendencies there were in this direction were weak, far weaker in Japan than in Germany, and in both were diverted and crushed. Though not the only cause, agrarian conditions and the specific types of capitalist transformation that took place in the countryside contributed very heavily to these defeats and the feebleness behind any impulse toward Western democratic forms.

There are certain forms of capitalist transformation in the countryside that may succeed economically, in the sense of yielding good profits, but which are for fairly obvious reasons unfavorable to the growth of free institutions of the nineteenth-century Western variety. Though

From Barrington Moore, Social Origins of Dictatorship and Democracy (*Boston, 1966*), pp. 433–52. Copyright 1966 by Barrington Moore. By permission of Beacon Press and Allen Lane, The Penguin Press.

these forms shade into each other, it is easy to distinguish two general types. A landed upper class may, as in Japan, maintain intact the pre-existing peasant society, introducing just enough changes in rural society to ensure that the peasants generate a sufficient surplus that it can appropriate and market at a profit. Or a landed upper class may devise wholly new social arrangements along the lines of plantation slavery. Straightforward slavery in modern times is likely to be the creation of a class of colonizing intruders into tropical areas. In parts of eastern Europe, however, indigenous nobilities were able to reintroduce serfdom, which reattached the peasants to the soil in ways that produced somewhat similar results. This was a halfway form between the two others.

Both the system of maintaining peasant society intact but squeezing more out of it and the use of servile or semiservice labor on large units of cultivation requires strong political methods to extract the surplus, keep the labor force in its place, and in general make the system work. Not all of these methods are of course political in the narrow sense. Particularly where the peasant society is preserved, there are all sorts of attempts to use traditional relationships and attitudes as the basis of the landlords' position. Since these political methods have important consequences, it will be helpful to give them a name. Economists distinguish between labor-intensive and capital-intensive types of agriculture, depending on whether the system uses large amounts of labor or capital. It may also be helpful to speak of labor-repressive systems, of which slavery is but an extreme type. The difficulty with such a notion is that one may legitimately ask precisely what type has not been labor-repressive. The distinction I am trying to suggest is one between the use of political mechanisms (using the term "political" broadly as just indicated) on the one hand and reliance on the labor market, on the other hand, to ensure an adequate labor force for working the soil and the creation of an agricultural surplus for consumption by other classes. Those at the bottom suffer severely in both cases.

To make the conception of a labor-repressive agricultural system useful, it would be well to stipulate that large numbers of people are kept at work in this fashion. It is also advisable to state explicitly what it does not include, for example, the American family farm of the mid-nineteenth century. There may have been exploitation of the labor of family members in this case, but it was done apparently mainly by the head of the household himself with minimal assistance from the outside. Again, a system of hired agricultural laborers where the workers had considerable real freedom to refuse jobs and move about, a condition rarely met in actual practice, would not fall under this rubric.

Finally, precommercial and preindustrial agrarian systems are not necessarily labor-repressive if there is a rough balance between the over-lord's contribution to justice and security and the cultivator's contribution in the form of crops. Whether this balance can be pinned down in any objective sense is a moot point best discussed in the following chapter when the issue arises in connection with the causes of peasant revolutions. Here we need only remark that the establishment of labor-repressive agrarian systems in the course of modernization does not necessarily produce greater suffering among the peasants than other forms. Japanese peasants had an easier time of it than did English ones. Our problem here is in any case a different one: how and why labor-repressive agrarian systems provide an unfavorable soil for the growth of democracy and an important part of the institutional complex leading to fascism.

In discussing the rural origins of parliamentary democracy,[1] we noticed that a limited degree of independence from the monarchy constituted one of the favorable conditions, though one that did not occur everywhere. While a system of labor-repressive agriculture may be started in opposition to the central authority, it is likely to fuse with the monarchy at a later point in search of political support. This situation can also lead to the preservation of a military ethic among the nobility in a manner unfavorable to the growth of democratic institutions. The evolution of the Prussian state constitutes the clearest example. Since we have referred to these developments at several points in this work,[2] it will be appropriate to sketch them very briefly here.

In northeastern Germany the manorial reaction of the fifteenth and sixteenth centuries, about which we shall have still more to say in quite another context, broke off the development toward the liberation of the peasantry from feudal obligations and the closely connected development of town life that in England and France eventually culminated in Western democracy. A fundamental cause was the growth of grain exports, though it was not the sole one. The Prussian nobility expanded its holdings at the expense of the peasantry which, under the Teutonic Order, had been close to freedom, and reduced them to serfdom. As part of the same process, the nobility reduced the towns to dependence by short-circuiting them with their exports. Afterward, the Hohenzollern rulers managed to destroy the independence of the nobility and crush the Estates, playing nobles and townsmen off against one another, thereby checking the aristocratic component in the move toward parliamentary government. The result in the seventeenth and eighteenth cen-

[1] Pp. 429–32.
[2] Pp. 420, 424.

turies was the "Sparta of the North," a militarized fusion of royal bureaucracy and landed aristocracy.[3]

From the side of the landed aristocracy came the conceptions of
inherent superiority in the ruling class and a sensitivity to matters of
status, prominent traits well into the twentieth century. Fed by new
sources, these conceptions could later be vulgarized and made appealing
to the German population as a whole in doctrines of racial superiority.
The royal bureaucracy introduced, against considerable aristocratic resistance, the ideal of complete and unreflecting obedience to an institution
over and above class and individual—prior to the nineteenth century
it would be anachronistic to speak of the nation. Prussian discipline,
obedience, and admiration for the hard qualities of the soldier come
mainly from the Hohenzollern efforts to create a centralized monarchy.

All this does not of course mean that some inexorable fate drove
Germany toward fascism from the sixteenth century onward, that the
process never could have been reversed. Other factors had to intervene,
some very important ones, as industrialization began to gather momentum during the nineteenth century. About these it will be necessary to
speak in a moment. There are also significant variants and substitutions
within the general pattern that has led to fascism, subalternatives one
might say if one wished to be very precise and technical, within the
major alternative of conservative modernization through revolution
from above. In Japan the notion of total commitment to authority
apparently came out of the feudal, rather than the monarchical, side of
the equation.[4] Again in Italy, where fascism was invented, there was no
powerful national monarchy. Mussolini had to go all the way back to
ancient Rome for the corresponding symbolism.

At a later stage in the course of modernization, a new and crucial
factor is likely to appear in the form of a rough working coalition between influential sectors of the landed upper classes and the emerging
commercial and manufacturing interests. By and large, this was a nineteenth-century political configuration, though it continued on into the
twentieth. Marx and Engels in their discussion of the abortive 1848 revolution in Germany, wrong though they were on other major features, put
their finger on this decisive ingredient: a commercial and industrial
class which is too weak and dependent to take power and rule in its
own right and which therefore throws itself into the arms of the landed
aristocracy and the royal bureaucracy, exchanging the right to rule for
the right to make money.[5] It is necessary to add that, even if the com-

[3] See Rosenberg, *Bureaucracy*; Carsten, *Origins of Prussia.*
[4] Sansom, *History of Japan*, I, 368.
[5] See Marx, *Selected Works*, II, "Germany: Revolution and Counter-Revolution,"
written mainly by Engels.

mercial and industrial element is weak, it must be strong enough (or soon become strong enough) to be a worthwhile political ally. Otherwise a peasant revolution leading to communism may intervene. This happened in both Russia and China after unsuccessful efforts to establish such a coalition. There also appears to be another ingredient that enters the situation somewhat later than the formation of this coalition: sooner or later systems of labor-repressive agriculture are liable to run into difficulties produced by competition from more technically advanced ones in other countries. The competition of American wheat exports created difficulties in many parts of Europe after the end of our Civil War. In the context of a reactionary coalition, such competition intensifies authoritarian and reactionary trends among a landed upper class that finds its economic basis sinking and therefore turns to political levers to preserve its rule.

Where the coalition succeeds in establishing itself, there has followed a prolonged period of conservative and even authoritarian government, which, however, falls far short of fascism. The historical boundaries of such systems are often somewhat blurred. At a rather generous estimate, one might hold that to this species belong the period from the Stein-Hardenberg reforms in Germany to the end of the First World War and, in Japan, from the fall of the Tokugawa Shogunate to 1918. These authoritarian governments acquired some democratic features: notably a parliament with limited powers. Their history may be punctuated with attempts to extend democracy which, toward the end, succeeded in establishing unstable democracies (the Weimar Republic, Japan in the twenties, Italy under Giolitti). Eventually the door to fascist regimes was opened by the failure of these democracies to cope with the severe problems of the day and reluctance or inability to bring about fundamental structural changes.[6] One factor, but only one, in the social anatomy of these governments has been the retention of a very substantial share in political power by the landed élite, due to the absence of a revolutionary breakthrough by the peasants in combination with urban strata.

Some of the semiparliamentary governments that arose on this basis carried out a more or less peaceful economic and political revolution from above that took them a long distance toward becoming modern industrial countries. Germany travelled the furthest in this direction, Japan only somewhat less so, Italy a great deal less, Spain very little. Now, in the course of modernization by a revolution from above, such

[6] Poland, Hungary, Rumania, Spain, and even Greece went through approximately this sequence. On the basis of admittedly inadequate knowledge, I would hazard the suggestion that much of Latin America remains in the era of authoritarian semi-parliamentary government.

a government has to carry out many of the same tasks performed elsewhere with the help of a revolution from below. The notion that a violent popular revolution is somehow necessary in order to sweep away "feudal" obstacles to industrialization is pure nonsense, as the course of German and Japanese history demonstrates. On the other hand, the political consequences from dismounting the old order from above are decidedly different. As they proceeded with conservative modernization, these semiparliamentary governments tried to preserve as much of the original social structure as they could, fitting large sections into the new building wherever possible. The results had some resemblance to present-day Victorian houses with modern electrical kitchens but insufficient bathrooms and leaky pipes hidden decorously behind newly plastered walls. Ultimately the makeshifts collapsed.

One very important series of measures was the rationalization of the political order. This meant the breakup of traditional and long established territorial divisions, such as the feudal *han* in Japan or independent states and principalities in Germany and Italy. Except in Japan, the breakup was not complete. But in the course of time a central government did establish strong authority and a uniform administrative system, and a more or less uniform law code and system of courts appeared. Again, in varying degrees, the state managed to create a sufficiently powerful military machine to be able to make the wishes of its rulers felt in the arena of international politics. Economically the establishment of a strong central government and the elimination of internal barriers to trade meant an increase in the size of the effective economic unit. Without such an increase in size, the division of labor necessary for an industrial society could not exist, unless all countries were willing to trade peacefully with one another. As the first country to industrialize, England had been able to draw on most of the accessible world for material and markets, a situation that gradually deteriorated during the nineteenth century when others caught up and sought to use the state to guarantee their markets and sources of supply.

Still another aspect of the rationalization of the political order has to do with the making of citizens in a new type of society. Literacy and rudimentary technical skills are necessary for the masses. Setting up a national system of education is very likely to bring on a conflict with religious authorities. Loyalty to a new abstraction, the state, must also replace religious loyalties if they transcend national boundaries or compete with one another so vigorously as to destroy internal peace. Japan had less of a problem here than Germany, Italy, or Spain. Yet even in Japan, as the somewhat artificial revival of *Shintō* indicates, there were substantial difficulties. In overcoming such difficulties, the existence of a foreign enemy can be quite useful. Then patriotic and conservative appeals to the military traditions of the landed aristocracy can overcome localist tendencies among this important group and push into the background any too insistent demands of the lower strata for an unwarranted share in the benefits of the new order.[7] In carrying out the task of rationalizing and extending the political order, these nineteenth-century governments were doing work that royal absolutism had already accomplished in other countries.

One striking fact about the course of conservative modernization is the appearance of a galaxy of distinguished political leaders: Cavour in Italy; in Germany, Stein, Hardenberg, and Bismarck, the most famous of them all; in Japan, the statesmen of the Meiji era. Though the reasons are obscure, it seems unlikely that the appearance of a similar leadership in similar circumstances could be pure coincidence. All were conservatives in the political spectrum of their time and country, devoted to the monarchy, willing and able to use it as an instrument of reform, modernization, and national unification. Though all were aristocrats, they were dissidents or outsiders of a sort in relation to the old order. To the extent that their aristocratic background contributed habits of command and a flair for politics, one may perhaps detect a contribution of the agrarian ancient régimes to the construction of a new society. But there were strong contrary pulls here too. To the extent that these men were aliens within the aristocracy, one may see the incapacity of this stratum to meet the challenge of the modern world merely with its own intellectual and political resources.

The most successful of the conservative regimes accomplished a great deal, not only in tearing down the old order but in establishing a new one. The state aided industrial construction in several important ways. It served as an engine of primary capitalist accumulation, gathering resources and directing them toward the building of an industrial plant. In the taming of the labor force it again played an important role, by no means entirely a repressive one. Armaments served as an important stimulus for industry. So did protectionist tariff policies. All of these measures at some point involved taking resources or people out of agriculture. Therefore they imposed from time to time a serious strain on the coalition between those sectors of the upper strata in business and in agriculture that was the main feature of the political system. Without the threat of foreign dangers, sometimes real, sometimes perhaps imaginary, sometimes as in the case of Bismarck deliberately manufactured

---

[7] Possibly one of the reasons the conservative Cavour had such difficulties with the relatively radical Garibaldi was the weakness of military traditions among the Italian landed aristocracy.

for domestic purposes, the landed interests might well have balked, to the point of endangering the whole process. The foreign threat alone, however, need not bear the whole weight of explaining this behavior.[8] Material and other rewards—the "payoff" in the language of gangsters and game theory—were quite substantial for both partners as long as they succeeded in keeping the peasants and industrial labor in place. Where there was substantial economic progress, the industrial workers were able to make significant gains, as in Germany, where *Sozialpolitik* was invented. It was in those countries that remained more backward, Italy to some extent, probably Spain to a greater extent, that there was more of a tendency to cannibalize the indigenous population.

Certain conditions seem to have been necessary for the successes of conservative modernization. First, it takes very able leadership to drag along the less perceptive reactionary elements, concentrated among, though not necessarily confined to, the landed upper classes. In the beginning, Japan had to suppress a real rebellion, the Satsuma revolt, to control these elements. Reactionaries can always advance the plausible argument that modernizing leaders are making changes and concessions that will merely arouse the appetites of the lower classes and bring on a revolution.[9] Similarly, the leadership must have at hand or be able to construct a sufficiently powerful bureaucratic apparatus, including the agencies of repression, the military and the police (compare the German saying *Gegen Demokraten helfen nur Soldaten*[10]), in order to free itself from the influence of both extreme reactionary and popular or radical pressures in the society. The government has to become separate from society, something that can happen rather more easily than simplified versions of Marxism would allow us to believe.

In the short run, a strong conservative government has distinct advantages. It can both encourage and control economic growth. It can see to it that the lower classes who pay the costs under all forms of modernization do not make too much trouble. But Germany and, even more, Japan were trying to solve a problem that was inherently insoluble, to modernize without changing their social structures. The only

---

[8] For a brilliant analysis of the situation in Germany toward the end of the nineteenth century see Kehr, *Schlachtflottenbau*. Weber, "Entwickelungstendenzen in der Lage der Ostelbischen Landarbeiter," in *Gesammelte Aufsätze*, esp. pp. 471–76, brings out very clearly the position of the Junkers.

[9] Such arguments were also very prominent in England as part of the reaction to the French Revolution. Many have been collected in Turberville, *House of Lords*. Tory reform could work in nineteenth-century England, however, at least partly because it was a sham battle anyway: the bourgeoisie had won, and only the more obtuse could fail to see their power.

[10] Only soldiers can help against democrats.

way out of this dilemma was militarism, which united the upper classes. Militarism intensified a climate of international conflict, which in turn made industrial advance all the more imperative, even if in Germany a Bismarck could for a time hold the situation in check, partly because militarism had not yet become a mass phenomenon. To carry out thoroughgoing structural reforms, i.e., to make the transition to a paying commercial agriculture without the repression of those who worked the soil and to do the same in industry, in a word, to use modern technology rationally for human welfare was beyond the political vision of these governments.[11] Ultimately these systems crashed in an attempt at foreign expansion, but not until they had tried to make reaction popular in the form of fascism.

Before discussing this final phase, it may be instructive to glance at unsuccessful reactionary trends in other countries. As mentioned above, this reactionary syndrome can be found at some point in all the cases I have examined. To see why it has failed in other countries may sharpen awareness of the reasons behind its successes. A brief look at these trends in such widely differing countries as England, Russia, and India may serve to bring out important underlying similarities concealed beneath a variety of historical experiences.

Beginning in the latter years of the French Revolution and lasting until about 1822, English society passed through a reactionary phase that recalls both the cases just discussed and contemporary problems of American democracy. During most of these years England was fighting against a revolutionary regime and its heirs, sometimes, it may have seemed, for national survival itself. As in our own time, the advocates of domestic reform were identified with a foreign enemy represented as the incarnation of all that was evil. Again, as in our own time, the violence, repressions, and betrayals of the revolutionary movement in France sickened and discouraged its English supporters, making easier and more plausible the work of reactionaries eager to stamp out the sparks that floated across the channel. Writing in the 1920s the great French historian Elie Halévy, certainly not a man given to dramatic exaggeration, asserted, "A reign of terror was established throughout England by the nobility and middle class—a terror more formidable,

---

[11] On this score, Germany and Japan are not of course unique. Since the Second World War, Western democracy has begun to display more and more of the same traits for broadly similar reasons that, however, no longer have much to do with agrarian questions. Somewhere Marx remarks that the bourgeoisie in its declining phase reproduces all the evils and irrationalities against which it once fought. So indeed did socialism in the effort to establish itself, thus allowing twentieth-century democracy to fly its muddy and blood-spattered banner of freedom with something short of outright cynical hypocrisy.

though more silent, than the noisy demonstrations [of the radicals]." [12] The events of the four decades and more that have passed since Halévy wrote these lines have dulled our senses and lowered our standards. No one writing now would be likely to refer to this phase as a reign of terror. The number of direct victims of repression was small. In the "massacre" of Peterloo (1819)—a derisive reference to Wellington's more famous victory of Waterloo—only eleven persons were killed. Nevertheless the gathering movement to reform Parliament was placed outside the law, the press muzzled, associations that smacked of radicalism forbidden, a rash of treason trials initiated, spies and *agents provocateurs* let loose among the people, the habeas corpus suspended *after* the war with Napoleon had ended. Repression and suffering were real and widespread, only partly mitigated by some continued articulate opposition: an aristocrat such as Charles James Fox (d. 1806) who spoke up courageously in Parliament, here and there a judge or a jury that refused to convict on treason or other charges.[13]

Why was this reactionary upsurge no more than a passing phase in England? Why did not England continue along this road to become another Germany? Anglo-Saxon liberties, Magna Charta, Parliament and such rhetoric will not do for an anwer. Parliament voted repressive measures by huge majorities.

An important part of the answer may be found in the fact that, a century before, certain extremist Englishmen had chopped off the head of their monarch to shatter the magic of royal absolutism in England. At a deeper level of causation, England's whole previous history, her reliance on a navy instead of an army, on unpaid justices of the peace instead of royal officials, had put in the hands of the central government a repressive apparatus weaker than that possessed by the strong continental monarchies. Thus the materials with which to construct a German system were missing or but feebly developed. Still, by now we have seen enough great social and political changes out of unpromising beginnings to suspect that the institutions could have been created if circumstances had been more favorable. But fortunately for human liberties they were not. The push toward industrialism had begun much earlier in England and was to render unnecessary for the English bour-

[12] Halévy, *History of the English People*, II, 19.

[13] An excellent and detailed description of what life was like for the lower classes in England during this period may be found in Thompson, *Making of Working Class*. The main governmental measures and some of their effects can be traced through Cole and Postgate, *British People*, pp. 132–34, 148–49, 157–59, 190–93. For some valuable additional details see Halévy, *History of the English People*, II, 23–25. Aristocratic opposition to repression may be found in Trevelyan, *History of England*, III, 89–92, and Turberville, *House of Lords*, pp. 98–100.

geoisie any great dependence on the crown and the landed aristocracy. Finally, the landed upper classes themselves did not need to repress the peasants. Mainly they wanted to get them out of the way in order to go over to commercial farming; by and large, economic measures would be enough to provide the labor force they needed. Succeeding economically in this particular fashion, they had little need to resort to repressive political measures to continue their leadership. Therefore in England manufacturing and agrarian interests competed with one another for popular favor during the rest of the nineteenth century, gradually extending the suffrage while jealously opposing and knocking down each other's more selfish measures (Reform Bill of 1832, abolition of the Corn Laws in 1846, gentry support for factory legislation, etc.).

In the English phase of reaction there were hints of fascist possibilities, particularly in some of the antiradical riots. But these were no more than hints. The time was still too early. Fascist symptoms we can see very much more clearly in another part of the world at a later point in time—during a brief phase of extremism in Russia after 1905. This was extreme even by Russian standards of the day; one could make a strong case for the thesis that Russian reactionaries invented fascism. Thus this phase of Russian history is especially illuminating because it shows that the fascist syndrome (1) can appear in response to the strains of advancing industrialism independently of a specific social and cultural background; (2) that it may have many roots in agrarian life; (3) that it appears partly in response to a weak push toward parliamentary democracy; (4) but cannot flourish without industrialism or in an overwhelmingly agrarian background—points, to be sure, all suggested by the recent histories of China and Japan too, though it is illuminating to find stronger confirmation in Russian history.

Shortly before the Revolution of 1905 the tiny Russian commercial and industrial class showed some signs of discontent with the repressive tsarist autocracy and a willingness to flirt with liberal constitutional notions. Workers' strikes, however, and the promise contained in the Imperial Manifesto of October 17, 1905, to meet some of the demands of the strikers, brought the industrialists safely back within the tsarist camp.[14] Against this background appeared the Black Hundreds movement. Drawing partly on American experience, they made "lynch" into a Russian word and asked for the application of *zakon lyncha*, lynch law. They resorted to violence in storm-trooper style to suppress "treason" and "sedition." If Russia could destroy the "kikes" and foreigners,

[14] Gitermann, *Geschichte Russlands*, III, 403, 409–10; Berlin, *Russkaya burzhuaziya*, pp. 226–27, 236.

their propaganda asserted, everyone could live happily in a return to "true Russian" ways. This anti-Semitic nativism had considerable appeal to backward, precapitalist, petty bourgeois elements in the cities and among the smaller nobility. However, in still backward peasant Russia of the early twentieth century, this form of rightist extremism was unable to find a firm popular basis. Among the peasants it succeeded mainly in areas of mixed nationality, where the explanation of all evil as being due to Jews and foreigners made some sense in terms of peasant experience.[15] As everyone knows, to the extent that they were politically active, the Russian peasants were revolutionary and eventually the major force in exploding the old regime.

In India, which is equally if not more backward, similar movements have likewise failed to obtain a firm basis among the masses. To be sure, Subhas Chandra Bose, who died in 1945, expressed dictatorial sentiments, worked for the Axis, and had a very large popular following. Though his fascist sympathies were consistent with other aspects of his public record and do not seem to be the outcome of momentary enthusiasm or opportunism, Subhas Chandra Bose has gone down in Indian tradition mainly as an extreme and perhaps misguided anti-British patriot.[16] There has also been a scattering of nativist Hindu political organizations, some of which developed the autocratic discipline of the European totalitarian party. They have reached the peak of their influence so far in the chaos and riots surrounding Partition, during which they helped to promote anti-Muslim riots and served as defense organs for Hindu communities against Muslim attacks, led, presumably, by similar organizations on the Muslim side. Their programs lack economic content and appear to be mainly a form of militant, xenophobic Hinduism, seeking to combat the stereotype that Hindus are pacific, divided by caste, and weak. So far their electoral appeal has been very small.[17]

One possible reason for the weakness of the Hindu variant of fascism to date may be the fragmentation of the Hindu world along caste, class, and ethnic lines. Thus a characteristically fascist appeal addressed to one segment would antagonize others, while a more general appeal, by taking on some color of universal panhumanism, begins to lose its fascist qualities. In this connection it is worth noticing that nearly all the extremist Hindu groups have opposed untouchability and other social dis-

[15] Levitskii, "Pravyya partii," *Obshchestvennoye dvizheniye v Rossii*, III, 347–472. See esp. pp. 432, 370–76, 401, 353–55.

[16] See Samra, "Subhas Chandra Bose," in Park and Tinker, eds., *Leadership and Political Institutions*, pp. 66–86, esp. pp. 78–79.

[17] Lambert, "Hindu Communal Groups," in Park and Tinker, eds., *Leadership and Political Institutions*, pp. 211–24.

abilities of caste.[18] The main reason, however, is probably the simple fact that Gandhi had already preempted the antiforeign and anticapitalist sentiment of huge masses of the population: peasants and artisans in the cottage industries. Under the conditions created by the British occupation, he was able to tie these sentiments to the interests of a large section of the business class. On the other hand, the landed élite generally stood aloof. Thus reactionary trends have been strong in India and have helped to delay economic progress since Independence. But as a mass phenomenon the larger movements belong to an historical species distinct from fascism.

Though it might be equally profitable to undertake a parallel consideration of democratic failures that preceded fascism in Germany, Japan, and Italy, it is enough for present purposes to notice that fascism is inconceivable without democracy or what is sometimes more turgidly called the entrance of the masses onto the historical stage. Fascism was an attempt to make reaction and conservatism popular and plebeian, through which conservatism, of course, lost the substantial connection it did have with freedom, some aspects of which were discussed in the preceding chapter.

The conception of objective law vanished under fascism. Among its most significant features was a violent rejection of humanitarian ideals, including any notion of potential human equality. The fascist outlook stressed not only the inevitability of hierarchy, discipline, and obedience, but also posited that they were values in their own right. Romantic conceptions of comradeship qualify this outlook but slightly; it is comradeship in submission. Another feature was the stress on violence. This stress goes far beyond any cold, rational appreciation of the factual importance of violence in politics to a mystical worship of "hardness" for its own sake. Blood and death often acquire overtones of erotic attraction, though in its less exalted moments fascism was thoroughly "healthy" and "normal," promising return to a cosy bourgeois, and even prebourgeois peasant, womb.[19]

Plebeian anticapitalism thus appears as the feature that most clearly distinguishes twentieth-century fascism from its predecessors, the nineteenth-century conservative and semiparliamentary regimes. It is a product of both the intrusion of capitalism into the rural economy and of strains arising in the postcompetitive phase of capitalist industry. Hence fascism developed most fully in Germany where capitalist industrial growth had gone the furthest within the framework of a conserva-

---

[18] Lambert, "Hindu Communal Groups," p. 219.

[19] To say that fascism was atavistic does not distinguish it sufficiently. So are revolutionary movements, as I have tried to show in some detail in the next chapter.

tive revolution from above. It came to light as only a weak secondary trend in such backward areas as Russia, China, and India. Prior to World War II, it failed to take much root in England and the United States where capitalism worked reasonably well or where efforts to correct its shortcomings could be attempted within the democratic framework and succeed with the help of a prolonged war boom. Most of the anticapitalist opposition to big business had to be shelved in practice, though one should not make the opposite error of regarding fascist leaders as merely the agents of big business. The attraction of fascism for the lower middle class in the cities, threatened by capitalism, has often been pointed out; here we may confine ourselves to a brief review of the evidence on its varying relationships to the peasantry in different countries. In Germany the effort to establish a massive conservative base in the countryside long antedates the Nazis. As Professor Alexander Gerschenkron points out, the basic elements of Nazi doctrine appear quite distinctly in the Junkers' generally successful efforts, by means of the Agrarian League established in 1894, to win the support of the peasants in non-Junker areas of smaller farms. *Führer* worship, the idea of a corporative state, militarism, anti-Semitism, in a setting closely related to the Nazi distinction between "predatory" and "productive" capital, were devices used to appeal to anticapitalist sentiments among the peasantry.[20] There are a good many indications that in subsequent years down to the depression the substantial and prosperous peasants were slowly losing ground to dwarf peasants. The depression constituted a deep and general crisis, to which the main rural response was National Socialism. Rural support for the Nazis came to an average of 37.4 percent, practically identical with that in the country as a whole in the last relatively free election of July 31, 1932.[21]

If one looks at a map of Germany showing the distribution of the Nazi vote in the rural areas and compares this map with others showing the distribution of land values, types of cultivation,[22] or of the areas of small, medium, and large farms,[23] the first impression will be that Nazism in

[20] *Bread and Democracy*, pp. 53, 55.

[21] For the rural vote see the map of Germany showing the distribution of Nazi voting for rural areas, July 1932, with *Stadtkreise* removed, in Loomis and Beegle, "Spread of German Nazism," p. 726. For the percentage of the Nazi vote in Germany as a whole, consult the election statistics from 1919 to 1933 assembled in Dittmann, *Das politische Deutschland.*

[22] Compare Loomis-Beegle map above with map inserts VIII, VIIIa, and I, in Sering, ed., *Deutsche Landwirtschaft.*

[23] Printed as appendices in *Statistik des Deutschen Reichs* and in less detail but on a single page as map insert IV in Sering, ed., *Deutsche Landwirtschaft.*

the countryside shows no consistent relationship with any of these. However, as one studies the maps more closely, one can discern substantial evidence to the effect that the Nazis succeeded most in their appeal to the peasant whose holding was relatively small and unprofitable *for the particular area in which it existed.*[24]

To the small peasant, suffering under the advance of capitalism with its problems of prices and mortgages that seemed to be controlled by hostile city middlemen and bankers, Nazi propaganda presented the romantic image of an idealized peasant, "the free man on free land." The peasant became the key figure in the ideology of the radical right as elaborated by the Nazis. The Nazis were fond of stressing the point that, for the peasant, land is more than a means with which to earn a living; it has all the sentimental overtones of *Heimat,* to which the peasant feels himself far more closely connected than the white-collar worker with his office or the industrial worker with his shop. Physiocratic and liberal notions found themselves jumbled together in these doctrines of the radical right.[25] "A firm stock of small and middle peasants," said Hitler in *Mein Kampf,* "has still been at all times the best protection against social evils as we have them now." Such a peasantry constitutes the only way through which a nation can secure its daily bread. He goes on, "Industry and commerce retreat from their unhealthy leading position and fit into the general framework of a national economy based on need and equality. Both are then no longer the basis for feeding the nation, but only a help in this." [26]

For our purposes there is nothing to be gained by examining the fate of these notions after the Nazis came to power. While a few starts were made here and there, most of them were junked because they contradicted the requirements of a powerful war economy, necessarily based

[24] Special studies too provide evidence for the view that the "little fellow" who was having a hard time of it under capitalist conditions was the one most receptive to the Nazi appeal. In Schleswig-Holstein the village communities where the Nazis won 80 to 100 percent of the vote were in what is known as the *Geest,* an area of small farms on poor soil, heavily dependent on sensitive markets for young cattle and hogs. On this, see Heberle, *Social Movements,* pp. 226, 228. Parts of Hannover show the same combination. Near Nuremberg, too, the Nazi vote ranged from 71 to 83 percent in an area of relatively low land values, middle-sized family farms, and generally marginal agriculture dependent on the urban market. See Loomis and Beegle, "Spread of German Nazism," pp. 726, 727. Further evidence pointing in the same direction is summarized and cited in Bracher, et al., *Machtergreifung,* 389–90.

[25] Bracher et al., *Machtergreifung,* pp. 390–91.

[26] *Mein Kampf,* pp. 151–52. For the main factual aspects of Nazi policy see also Schweitzer, "Nazification," in *Third Reich,* pp. 576–94.

on industry. The notion of a retreat from industry was only the most obviously absurd feature.[27]

In Japan, as in Germany, pseudoradical anticapitalism gained a considerable foothold among the Japanese peasantry. There too the original impulse came from the landed upper classes. On the other hand, its more extreme forms, such as the assassins' bands among junior military officers, though they claimed to speak for the peasants, do not seem to have had a strong following among them. Extremism was in any case absorbed into the more general framework of "respectable" Japanese conservatism and military aggression, for which the peasantry provided a mass basis. . . .

Italian fascism displays the same pseudoradical and propeasant features found in Germany and Japan. In Italy, on the other hand, these notions were more of an opportunistic growth, a cynical decoration put on to take advantage of circumstances. Cynical opportunism was present in Germany and Japan too, of course, but seems to have been much more blatant in Italy.

Immediately after the 1914 war, there was a bitter struggle in the north Italian countryside between Socialist and Christian-Democratic trade unions on the one hand and the big landowners on the other. At this point, i.e., 1919–20, Mussolini, according to Ignazio Silone, paid no attention to the countryside, did not believe in a fascist conquest of the land, and thought fascism would always be an urban movement.[28] But the struggle between the landowners and the unions, representing the interests of hired labor and tenants, gave fascism an unexpected opportunity to fish in troubled waters. Presenting themselves as the saviors of civilization against Bolshevism, *fasci*—bands of idealists, demobilized army officers, and just plain toughs—broke up rural union headquarters, often with the connivance of the police, and during 1921 destroyed the leftist movement in the countryside. Among those who streamed into fascist ranks were peasants who had climbed into the middle ranks of landowners, and even tenants who hated the monopolistic practices of the union.[29] During the summer of this year Mussolini made his famous observation that "if Fascism does not wish to die or, worse still, to commit suicide, it must now provide itself with a doctrine. . . . I do wish that during the two months which are still to elapse be-

[27] For the fate of the agrarian program, consult Wunderlich, *Farm Labor*, pt. III, "The Period of National Socialism."
[28] Silone, *Fascismus*, p. 107.
[29] Schmidt, *Plough and Sword*, pp. 34–38; Silone, *Fascismus*, p. 109; Salvemini, *Fascist Dictatorship*, pp. 67, 73.

fore our National Assembly meets, the philosophy of Fascism could be created." [30]

Only later did Italian fascist leaders begin to declare that fascism was "ruralizing" Italy, championing the cause of the peasants, or that it was primarily a "rural phenomenon." These claims were nonsense. The number of owner operators dropped by 500,000 between 1921 and 1931; that of cash-and-share tenants rose by about 400,000. Essentially fascism protected big agriculture and big industry at the expense of the agricultural laborer, small peasant, and consumer. [31]

As we look back at fascism and its antecedents, we can see that the glorification of the peasantry appears as a reactionary symptom in both Western and Asiatic civilization at a time when the peasant economy is facing severe difficulties. . . . To say that such ideas are merely foisted on the peasants by the upper classes is not true. Because the ideas find an echo in peasant experience, they may win wide acceptance, the wider, it seems, the more industrialized and modern the country is.

As evidence against the evaluation that such glorification constitutes a reactionary symptom, one might be tempted to cite Jefferson's praise of the small farmer and John Stuart Mill's defense of peasant farming. Both thinkers, however, in the characteristic fashion of early liberal capitalism, were defending not so much peasants as small independent property owners. There is in their thought none of the militant chauvinism and glorification of hierarchy and submission found in the later versions, though there are occasional overtones of a romantic attitude toward rural life. Even so, their attitude toward agrarian problems and rural society does indicate the limits that liberal thinkers had reached at their respective points in time. For such ideas to serve reactionary purposes in the twentieth century, they have had to take on a new coloring and appear in a new context; the defense of hard work and small property in the twentieth century has an entirely different political meaning from what it had in the middle of the nineteenth or the latter part of the eighteenth centuries.

[30] Quoted by Schmidt, *Plough and Sword*, pp. 39–40.
[31] For figures and details see Schmidt, *Plough and Sword*, v, 132–34, 66–67, 71, 113.

Ernst Nolte

FASCISM AS AN ANTIMODERNIST REVOLT

Ernst Nolte (b. 1923) is a German scholar who came to the study of history after training in philosophy. He is Professor of European History at Marburg University. Nolte is concerned with understanding fascism rather than recording its history and his effort to reestablish the Hegelian unity of history and philosophy is related to the "underlying assumption" of his work, that "the fascist era claimed more victims than any era in history, and for this very reason demands the utmost intellectual effort at understanding."

The writer who at the end of the nineteenth century had proposed calling his own time the "era of imperialism" would not have found many to agree with him. Yet the term had been in use for centuries and, in spite of many different interpretations, possessed a relatively clearly defined meaning as to content and scope. This does not apply to the term "fascism," with the result that the phrase "era of fascism" does not find ready acceptance even today.

In 1920 the word "fascism" was known to very few people in Europe, and even Mussolini placed it between quotation marks as being a neologism. In 1923, however, the leftist parties throughout Germany staged an "antifascist day," thereby demonstrating as forcefully against the German, Hungarian, and Bulgarian "Fascists" as against Mussolini's victorious Blackshirts. A particular interpretation of the term was an essential before Hitler's seizure of power—that notorious description of the Social Democrats as Social Fascists, with which the Communist party of Germany repeated the fatal mistake of the Italian Communists

From Ernst Nolte, Three Faces of Fascism (New York, 1966), pp. 3–8, 11–12, 20–21, 25–26, 419–24, 429–30. Translated by Leila Vennewitz. Copyright © 1963 by R. Piper & Co. Verlag, Munich. Trans. copyright 1965 by R. Piper & Co. Verlag, Munich. Reprinted by permission of Holt, Rinehart and Winston, Inc., and Weidenfeld and Nicholson, Ltd.

in extended and crasser form. But at about the same time the leaders of certain groups of the extreme Right proposed to call an "antifascist congress." A kind of compromise between the former very wide and the latter very narrow definition was represented, after the great about-face of the Comintern, by the commonly held concept of antifascism which made the policy of the Popular Fronts possible and under whose banners the great world coalition finally fought against Hitler and Mussolini, although this coalition had certainly not been formed under these banners. Today the concept of fascism is still one of direct political significance. The question of whether or not the Franco regime can be called fascist touches upon national interests, and a whole series of new developments has led to a notable revival of the term.

To inquire into the nature of the "era of fascism," then, means to add the specific problem of a still much-disputed term—the scholarly discussion of which has barely begun—to the overall difficulty which every periodization entails. On the other hand, it is obvious that the question of fascism cannot be separated from the question of its era, since no universally acknowledged and meaningful concept of the era between 1919 and 1945 exists. Even if the term "fascism" is taken strictly as a name, that is, to describe an isolated phenomenon, the question remains of the extent to which events in Italy were *not*—in spite of their incalculable world-wide effect—epochal. Whichever way we look at it, the common nature of the inquiry into fascism and the era is inescapable, and it is our task to define the concepts and review the facts.

However, the order in which the thematic material is placed is governed by one helpful limitation. Even though fascism existed after 1945 and has continued to exist since that time, and even though it is still capable of arousing bitter conflicts, it cannot be said to have real significance as far as the image of the era is concerned unless the term be stripped almost entirely of its traditional connotation. Thus the very subject of this study precludes any reference to events of the present day.

Hand in hand with this limitation goes a very tangible advantage; for contemporary history, in so many respects at a disadvantage when compared with its older sisters, has at its disposal a virtually ready-made division of eras, enabling us to trace the course of fascism deductively.

To use the term "era of the world wars" and imply the period from 1914 to 1945 would certainly not be valid for all time; but seen from the present day, the dates of August 1, 1914, and May 8, 1945, represent such profound cleavages in history that their epoch-making character has never been denied. What is disputed (aside from how to divide the subsections) is the context into which the epoch is to be placed and the point in time at which the cataclysmic caesura represented by the outbreak of war caused the new constellations to mature and acquire their first self-awareness. The most important of these concepts imply an answer to the question, whether the chronological and formal criterion might not be augmented by a more meaningful one. It should be enough to enumerate three of the best-known of these concepts:

1. The era of the world wars forms part of an age of revolutions and profound social changes, an age of which the most visible starting point was the French revolution.

2. The immediate roots of this era are to be found in the period of imperialism. It was during this time that all the conflicts developed which merely achieved their climax with the outbreak of war.

3. It was not until 1917 that World War I ceased to be simply a conflict of national states. With the entry of the United States into the war and the Bolshevik revolution, the constellation became a universal one: a general state of civil war and the future splitting of the world into two are already discernible in outline.

From each of these definitions and interpretations it is possible to derive the concept of a new type of political phenomenon.

None of the major political trends in Europe had evolved from a war: liberalism was the expression of the rise of the bourgeoisie; conservatism originally represented the reaction of the threatened aristocratic ruling class; socialism belonged to the proletariat born of the process of industrialization. None of these political doctrines wanted a world war or gave it its unqualified blessing after the outbreak. It was the war that made room for a political phenomenon, which was, so to speak, its very own child, a child which by innate law strove in turn to engender yet another war.

Since 1789, despite all reaction and many political defeats, the social revolution had spread inexorably throughout Europe. It led the bourgeoisie almost everywhere to participate in political power and raised it to a position from which it exerted a determining influence on society; it also provided the bourgeoisie with a new adversary in the shape of the socialistic proletariat. On all sides the newly emancipated class joined forces with the old ruling class against the approaching menace. Although this alliance was only a pragmatic and temporary one, small groups were beginning to transform it into one of principle even before 1914: a historically unique marriage between aristocratic conviction and plebeian reality. At first these groups remained small and unnoticed, but under certain conditions the principle on which they were founded could be of significance for the future since this principle corresponded to a basic characteristic of the social revolution itself: namely, that new auxiliary troops were continually joining the counterrevolution from the ranks of the emancipated, with the result that its face was changing as constantly as that of the revolution.

Before 1914 what was known as imperialism showed itself everywhere to be a compromise between the banal egoism of the national states and the more elusive requirements of the liberal and socialist traditions. Neither Cecil Rhodes nor Theodore Roosevelt nor Friedrich Naumann had any other object in view than to extend their respective "cultural ideas" of their time to the advantage and for the salvation of all peoples within their scope. But was it not implicit in the fundamental nature of this imperialism that it bestow unquestioning approval upon itself?

There is no doubt that the year 1917 represented a cleavage which cut deep into its own time and far into the future. But it is equally certain that the two great powers whose emergence was marked by this cleavage soon withdrew to their own native ground. When the American people opted against Wilson in 1920 it chose two decades of a new isolationism; the skepticism Lenin felt toward the "workers' aristocracy" of the West was soon confirmed. It turned out that the victory of bolshevism in Russia did not prevent its defeat on all the social battlefields of Europe, if it did not in fact actually cause it. Starting not later than 1923, the year of the failure of the last revolts in Germany, the Communist parties were operating everywhere more to the advantage of their enemies' cause than to their own. The Soviet Union became once more an unknown country on the periphery of the world, and Europe was once more the arena of world events. But was it likely that after that fearful interlude the participants should remain quite the same?

The war, the revolution, imperialism, the emergence of the Soviet Union and the United States, were not locally confined phenomena. Neither could a movement which came into being as an outcome of the war, a movement which fought revolution with revolutionary methods, which radicalized imperialism, and which saw in the Soviet Union (and in "Americanism" too, although with less emphasis) the greatest of all threats, be called a locally confined phenomenon, no matter how many differences might be attributable to it due to local conditions. This movement would have found its place in the Europe of the postwar period even if Mussolini and Hitler had never lived. No term other than "fascism" has ever been seriously proposed for it. This word has the drawback of being simultaneously name and concept; it has the advantage of being without concrete content and of not, like German National Socialism, implying an unjustifiable claim. It is not the business of scholarly investigation to invent a new term just because the one commonly used cannot satisfy all requirements.

If, then, fascism can be defined as a new reality which did not exist before World War I, or only in rudimentary form, the obvious next step is to declare it to be the characteristic political trend of an era in which, owing to the withdrawal of the two recently emerged "flanking powers," Europe can be regarded once more as the focal point of the world. Out of four principal powers in this Europe two, as we know, became fascist within ten years, and after ten more years a continent which had become almost totally fascist (or so, at least, it seemed) had torn the two "flanking powers" from their isolation and challenged them to battle.

When a historian speaks of the "era of the Counter Reformation" he does not imply that the Counter Reformation was the dominant force in all areas of the then known world and that it met with no resistance, nor is he obliged to believe that it contained the seeds of the future. He does not even have to regard it as "necessary." In order to describe a period marked by powerful religious elements he simply uses the religious phenomenon which, being central to this trend, represented its most novel and thus most typical manifestation. In the same way, if we are to name an era marked by political conflicts after the most novel phenomenon in the center of events, we cannot do otherwise than call the era of the world wars an era of fascism.

This definition of the era is not new, and so should not be surprising. At various times it has been used (explicitly or implicitly) by leading representatives of the most disparate parties.

At the peak of his reputation and independence during the years 1930 to 1935, Mussolini often said that fascist ideas were the ideas of the age and that within a few years the whole of Europe would be fascist. On all sides he descried, it seemed to him, "fascist ferments of the political and spiritual renewal of the world"; he defined fascism as "organized, concentrated, authoritarian democracy on a national basis," and did not hesitate to claim for it anything in the world that demanded a strengthening of state power and intervention in the economy.

Mussolini's theory of the imminent fascistization of the world undoubtedly seems prejudiced and vague. Yet Thomas Mann's remarks in his essay *Dieser Friede* ("This Peace"), written at the height of the controversy following Munich from the opposite point of view, are very similar. He speaks of the "complete victory" of the "massive trends of the times which can be summarized in the word fascism" and traces them to "Europe's psychological preparedness for fascist infiltration in a political, moral, and intellectual respect." A little later he calls fascism "a disease of the times which is at home everywhere and from which no country is free." And even after Hitler's defeat he speaks (in his discourse on Nietzsche) of "the fascist era of the Occident in which we live and, despite the military victory over fascism, will long continue to live."

This is somewhat reminiscent of the theory expounded by Georg Lukács in his book, *Die Zerstörung der Vernunft*. Here he attempts to describe philosophical irrationalism as an essential component of and background to National Socialism, as the "reactionary answer to the great problems of the past hundred and fifty years." On Germany's path "from Schelling to Hitler" is to be found practically every name of any stature in German philosophy after Hegel's death: Schopenhauer and Nietzsche, Dilthey and Simmel, Scheler and Heidegger, Jaspers and Max Weber. However, in contrast to many attempts at analysis (particularly in Anglo-Saxon literature), Lukács sees the spiritual foundation of National Socialism as other than exclusively German: he regards the evolution in Germany's intellectual and political life merely as the most prominent manifestation of an international process within the capitalist world.

Of course there are many objections to Lukács' ideas, but this much is undoubtedly true: namely, that, beginning with the close of the nineteenth century, a change took place in the spiritual climate all over Europe, a change which was bound to further—although not create—a new political orientation disaffiliating itself from, and indeed directly opposing, the traditional political environment. With no immediate relevance to the political events of the day, the Nietzschean doctrine, which alone permitted the equation of socialism, liberalism, and traditional conservatism, was adopted and developed by a circle of fascistoid authors: the doctrine of the revolt of the slaves and of the impoverishment of life through Judeo-Christian resentment.

A no less convincing proof of the epochal nature of fascism is the fact that it exerted the strongest possible influence on its opponents. This is true not primarily in the narrow sense that it imposed its own traits directly upon them: in this we are often faced with a matter of parallel developments (although they, too, are of great consequence in forming opinion). Fascism forced its adversaries to undertake the most painful self-reappraisal in generations, for it was in their attitude toward fascism that they committed their direst errors and misjudgments.

What was antifascism in its earliest form—the opposition of the Aventine after the murder of Matteotti—if not the alliance of those who before the March on Rome had been unable to agree and had thereby suffered defeat? What did the slogan "antifascist united front" launched by the communists after 1935 mean, if not the most revolutionary revision of their own tactics of the previous decade? What, on their highest level, was the content of the discussions and writings of German emigrants, if not the most critical self-examination of the German mentality ever to have taken place? And was not this self-examination at times compelled to admit that the very opposition to fascism often bore fascist traits? . . .

In 1919 war and revolution in Europe were more closely contiguous than ever before or since, and that year signaled the starting point of the first fascist parties. Their development progressed at varying speeds, but the years 1922 and 1923 were crucial way stations. During these years the first two fascist parties entered the spotlight of history and world-wide interest; it was chiefly these two which were to keep the world in suspense: one of them achieved a momentous victory, the other suffered a still more momentous defeat. At the end of October, 1922, Mussolini's Blackshirts conquered the capital with their curious "March on Rome," and barely more than a year later Hitler ran impetuously against the reluctantly drawn sword of a government that until then had been consistently friendly and favorably inclined.

A third event from this period is worthy of mention, although it took place in a corner of Europe. On June 9, 1923, the government of the peasant leader Aleksandr Stamboliski—called by his enemies an "agrarian communist"—was overthrown in Sofia, and the new government of Tsankov steered a bloody course of oppression against the smoldering peasant resistance and in particular against the Communist party. By June 23 the Comintern had issued an appeal to the workers of the world, calling upon them to protest against the crimes of the "victorious Bulgarian fascist clique." Thus in 1922–23 the world saw not only the emergence of the two principal fascist movements under the sign of what was, compared to 1919, a strangely altered battle front, but also the first official appearance of that polemical and universal interpretation which was so vital to the further development of fascism.

From then on fascist movements mushroomed in Europe. In most cases it is hardly possible to say to what extent independent causes or the influence of Mussolini's shining example stood godfather at their birth. . . .

FIRST DEFINITION

Superficial though it may be, this survey of the phenomenon and its interpretations to date enables us to arrive at a preliminary definition which will serve as a guide and at the same time be subjected to study and demonstration within this analysis.

Neither antiparliamentarianism nor anti-Semitism is a suitable criterion for the concept of fascism. It would be equally imprecise to define fascism as anticommunism, but it would be obviously misleading to use a definition which did not adequately stress, or even entirely omitted, this basis criterion. Nevertheless, the identifying conception must also be taken into account. Hence the following suggests itself:

Fascism is anti-Marxism which seeks to destroy the enemy by the evolvement of a radically opposed and yet related ideology and by the use of almost identical and yet typically modified methods, always, however, within the unyielding framework of national self-assertion and autonomy.

This definition implies that without Marxism there is no fascism, that fascism is at the same time closer to and further from communism than is liberal anticommunism, that it necessarily shows at least an inclination toward a radical ideology, that fascism should never be said to exist in the absence of at least the rudiments of an organization and propaganda comparable to those of Marxism. It enables us to understand the extent to which there can be stages of fascism: according to the evolution of the ideology and the predominance of one of its two chief components, the pseudosocialist or the elite—that is, race—element; according to the degree of determination in, and the more or less universal nature of, the will to destruction; and according to the energy of execution. The decisive factors, however, are starting point and direction, for this concept is a "teleological" one, and even the most marked differentiation of stages does not do away with the unity of its essential nature.

Finally, this definition enables us to make concrete distinctions and identifications: neither the Pan-Germans nor Stoecker's Christian Socialists come under it; on the other hand, there is no reason to maintain that every opponent of Hitler in his party or in the other groups of the extreme right was a non-Fascist. . . .

But we must turn to a serious shortcoming. The fact that the "intellectual climate" within which fascism and National Socialism grew up cannot be portrayed in detail is unavoidable. Such writers as Oswald Spengler and Carl Schmitt, Gottfried Benn and Ernst Jünger, are complex figures, and their relationship to fascism is obscure and in any case ineffective. If our study is not to degenerate into the uncertain and the inconclusive, we must limit it strictly to outright political phenomena. But fascism is also underestimated as a political phenomenon if we allow it to originate with World War I, out of nothing or at best a few literary precursors. The political constellations of the postwar period were anticipated by two decades in the politically most advanced and turbulent country in Europe when the conservative groups in the Dreyfus affair suffered a serious defeat and saw the state in the hands of leftist-oriented forces, which elsewhere in Europe were still in a situation of hopeless opposition, whereas at the same time liberal and socialist ideas had reached a crisis and the war was casting a shadow that for receptive minds was sufficiently noticeable. The Action Française was the first political grouping of any influence or intellectual status to bear unmistakably fascist traits. The fact that it appeared as the latest form of the oldest counterrevolutionary movement—French legitimism and royalism—is its most revealing characteristic, for those modern traits which cannot be traced to this tradition stand out all the more clearly. It goes without saying that its monarchism is not enough to distinguish it irrevocably from fascism: Codreanu and Mosley, De Bono and Ernst Röhm, were also supporters of the monarchy. However, it is not intended as a proof of positive equation with fascism if one long section is devoted to the Action Française and placed at the head of this study. It will probably show that the Action Française should be called early fascism and that from certain points of view it is even more closely akin to National Socialism than to Italian fascism.

The precursor here is not the narrow world of anti-Semitic writers, but the great and significant tradition of French counterrevolutionary thought in all its manifestations. That which in National Socialism seems narrow, in Italian fascism too limited to a particular period, stands revealed here on a broader horizon. The curious *volte face* in liberal thought to be found in Renan and Taine offers more than a mere substitute for the lack of German fascistoid authors. In this *volte face*—more convincingly because more hesitantly than in the case of Nietzsche— we can grasp that change which, intellectually speaking, anticipated the era of the world wars by nearly half a century.

The history of the Action Française forms a symptomatic component of the history of a country which from 1789 to 1919 was always politically a few steps ahead of the rest of Europe.

In spite of all its doctrinal rigidity, the system of Maurras' ideas is of an extent, acuteness, and depth without parallel in the Germany or Italy of that time.

The practice of the Action Française anticipates, in the clear simplicity of the rudimentary, the characteristic traits of the infinitely cruder and more wholesale methods used in Italy and Germany.

Seen by itself, the Action Française is not an epochal phenomenon. Yet it is, as it were, the missing link demonstrating fascism as a stage in an overall and much older struggle. . . .

NATURE AND ANTINATURE

Once again, before proceeding to the final definition it is as well to pause for a moment. Attention should first be turned to those instances in which Hitler's thinking attains a level of marked generality, such as where he speaks of "nature."

The main features of his doctrine are well known: life is a struggle in which the stronger prevails and thus does nature's bidding, for nature has given life to her creatures for the purpose of eternal struggle to ensure a rising evolution rather than a general putrefaction.

These are banalities; the point is to discover what meaningful conceptions might be hidden in them. It must therefore be asked: *Who* is struggling, *what* kind of a struggle is it, *why* must it be emphasized?

First of all, what Hitler quite obviously always has in mind is a struggle of human beings against other human beings. Every example he cites from nature has but one purpose: to illustrate the essence of this struggle. The exemplification, however, is highly revealing. Every animal mates with one of its own kind, he says at the beginning of the chapter on "People and Race" in *Mein Kampf*. Titmouse pairs off with titmouse, finch with finch, stork with stork; the species are strictly separated, and there is no such thing as a fox with humane impulses toward geese, or a cat with friendly feelings toward mice. Hitler's intention is obvious: he equates (human) race with (animal) species, thus attempting on the one hand to create unbridgeable gulfs between people, and on the other to force the individual human being inextricably into his race, which thereby becomes the supreme and sole motivation for his actions. Hitler is very fond of comparing human beings with animals or objects. A German is under no compulsion to let himself be devoured by Jews, just as a tiger cannot help eating people. Apes trample individualists in their herds to death for being antisocial—the same rule should apply to human beings. "Tough as leather, swift as a greyhound, hard as Krupp steel"—that is what the man of the coming Reich will be like. This leads to apparently quite serious theses of sectarian fanaticism; comparison with the life phases of dogs shows that man eats the wrong kind of food, his normal life span should be a hundred and forty to a hundred and eighty years; or: apes are vegetarians and point to the right way for mankind. Hence the subjects of the struggle are closely knit races or racial power-structures (nations). This is what Hitler meant when he said: "God created peoples but not classes."

The distinguishing mark of this struggle is war. Hitler obviously meant this when he said: "One creature drinks the blood of another. The death of one nourishes the other. One should not drivel about humane feelings. . . . The struggle goes on." Its result will decide who shall be master and who shall be slave. For Hitler, no other sociological categories existed. That is why for him there are "only conquerors and serfs," that is why a people of fifteen million cannot hope to be anything but the "slaves . . . of others."

Hitler usually defined his purpose as the preservation of the species, frequently also as the selective breeding and improvement of mankind. Emphasis is entirely on the first definition; where it is not a case of a pseudoliberal residue, the second must be understood as proceeding from the first.

This is Hitler's world of eternal struggle in which all who live must fight; war to decide hegemony or slavery between the races as the ultimate and supreme eternal fact of life. And this is the heart of his religious message, to which he wanted to devote all his time after the victory: "Unconditional submission to the divine law of existence," devout regard for the "fundamental necessity of the rule of nature."

But why preach what is self-evident? Does "nature" perhaps have an enemy, that one must go to her defense? Indeed! There is for Hitler also something which "detaches [mankind] from the instinct of nature." Sometimes he calls it semieducation, sometimes materialist science; cause and agent in his eyes is always the Jew. Man might think that he can "correct nature," that he is something more than a bacillus on the planet. "Pathological ideas of cowardly know-alls and critics of nature" can cause man to regard himself as the "lord of creation," that is, exempt from its fundamental laws. Then a people can lose its sound instinct that it must acquire land by force of arms. Then the Jew can open the "breach" within the people itself and invent a social problem to disrupt the people's unity. Then the intellectuals come to the fore with their uncertain instincts and their vacillation. Then the Jewish-Christian work of antinature is complete. Then the nation stands on the brink of annihilation. For it seems there is an innate peril in man himself, a root of disease, a sword of antinature: "Man alone, of all living creatures, attempts to transgress the laws of nature."

The Führer and the movement snatch the race back from the brink, and force it once more onto nature's path. As the vanguard of the "cruel queen of all wisdom," at the eleventh hour they take up the battle against antinature, whose tool is the Jewish people, for "the German people is the typical land-rooted people, the Jewish is the typical landless people." Primordial principles themselves confront each other here; the only alternative is victory or extinction—and this decides the fate of the world.

No further quotations are needed to make it clear what is meant by saying that the power of "antinature" fills Hitler with dread: it is this "going beyond" in human nature which is capable of transforming the essence of human order and relations—transcendence. What Hitler— and not only Hitler—feels to be threatened are certain basic structures of social existence. He too—like Maurras—is afraid *of* man *for* man. But he did not only think, he acted. And in his actions he carried his principle to its final and utmost logical conclusion and at the same time to its irrevocable end. Hence it is possible to define Hitler's radical fascism, which called itself "National Socialism," as follows:

National Socialism was the death throes of the sovereign, martial, inwardly antagonistic group. It was the practical and violent resistance to transcendence.

The parallelism of Hitler's and Maurras' thinking is remarkable, even —and especially—in those points where Hitler crudely simplifies Maurras' subtlety or clearly exposes his contradictions. The light each throws on the other substantiates whatever appears to be speculative in this definition. That Maurras' whole thought represents a resistance to transcendence and unconditional defense of the autarkic-sovereign, martial, aristocratic state of the ancien régime as a paradigm for France for all time, can hardly be doubted. It has been shown that Maurras was not really a man of the ancien régime, and that it was perhaps only from his perspective that he could so clearly emphasize those traits. Nevertheless, he was infinitely closer to his paradigmatic epoch than Hitler was to his and had a far more concrete conception of it. Hitler thought in peasant-soldier categories—yet between him and the peasant-soldier nature there yawned an unbridgeable gulf. He mythicized the fear of bolshevism of the ruling classes—yet he felt nothing but hatred and contempt for those classes. He correctly perceived the relationship between science and "antinature"—yet again and again he displaced the crassest features of a scientific and enlightened age. He was so far removed spiritually from all the phenomena he championed that it has frequently and justifiably been suspected that he was driven by nothing but the pure will to power. One has only to look at the changeless basic traits of his thoughts and emotions to see the error of this view; but this much of it remains correct: that it was precisely his curious and uncanny detachment that enabled Hitler to uncover the naked basic structures of each phenomenon.

Sovereign is any group which in practice lives independently of others. Through the ages, lack of communication alone has permitted innumerable groups to exist in a state of only nominally restricted sovereignty and quite a few in a state of actually unrestricted sovereignty.

Martial is what every such group must be that is subject to threat from outside. The variety of circumstances produces numerous levels in history ranging from an out-and-out warrior-state to a peaceful insular existence. But the second possibility is an imperfect manifestation of the first and unfailingly attributable to especially favorable conditions.

Inwardly antagonistic is any group which in circumstances of essential shortages is stratified according to occupation or class, with the result that certain members of society are excluded from full participation in the material and spiritual benefits of the community, either in principle or in fact. Apart from the hypothetical communist primordial society, this was more or less the case with all hitherto existing groups, while here too the more radical manifestation of a strictly hierarchically organized society has claim to priority.

The first two characteristics proceed logically from the concept of the particular society. The third can be derived from the concept of differentiation and can in any case be demonstrated everywhere in the field of historical experience.

Sovereignty, endorsement of active war, and internal antagonism may therefore be considered basic characteristics of *all* hitherto existing human societies. However, it is an insight of the most crucial importance that people *never* derived their self-image exclusively or even principally from this reality of their existence, at least since the emergence of the great redemptive religions.

No matter how independent a Christian state may have been, it always ascribed ultimate sovereignty to God alone. No matter how belligerent a Moslem warrior may have been, he always related his deeds to a transcendental realm of peace. Although in Buddhist states social differences may have been crasser than elsewhere, the servants of the prevailing religion relegated them by example and doctrine to a transitory level.

In all great societies throughout history, a universal doctrine and a particular reality have always lived in a precarious symbiosis. From a certain level of consciousness on, nothing could be more convincing than to call this symbiosis a lie, and to declare the doctrine to be an ideological transfiguration of the imperfect and odious reality.

With the growth of bourgeois society and the emergence of the liberal philosophies, a conception arose in Europe which regarded the elimination of the particular reality as well as of the ideological "superstructure" as possible. It sought to replace them with a universal society which would dispense certainly with war and if possible with internal antagonism.

It is now all-important to recognize that National Socialism is not an ideology for the very reason that it aims ruthlessly at opposing the liberal and Marxist doctrine of the realization of the universal nature of man. Hence its *Weltanschauung* consists essentially in accusing all ideologies in the traditional sense of demoralizing tendencies because they introduce a germ of disintegration into the blood-rooted unity of the race and infect the original healthy state with a virus. In its positive sense, therefore, the National Socialist doctrine is not at all that—possibly mendacious—invocation of a superior good, a universal purpose: it is in a very primitive way a mere "legend" which seeks, by alluding to better blood, not so much to legitimize as to establish the rule of the rulers in the eyes of the subjugated.

Consequently, fascism is the first phenomenon after the long epoch of ideological history in which the particular reality seeks itself and only itself (although with varying degrees of clarity in the different manifestations of fascism). Now for the first time its fundamental structures attain a definite self-awareness. But they only become aware of that which is no longer self-evident. Where the real desires itself for its own sake, it is about to elude itself and thus plunges into its *death throes*.

Moreover, it is not only a deduction of this kind but the reality of history since 1945 which justifies the term "death throes." Hitler's death did not in any sense mean that the world had seen the last of sovereignty and the claim to it; but even the two great powers of our day do not seek it as such and for all time. The thesis that the war of aggression of one of the powers would entail its own destruction is equivalent to the realization that unconditional particular sovereignty is today neither possible nor desirable.

This is certainly not to imply that war has ceased to be an ever-present threat. But now no one dares extol it for its own sake: not because man is better, but because war has become more potent, too potent for man. There are still soldiers, and they are indispensable, but for the first time in history it is not permissible for them to desire the active execution of their occupation.

Nor does it mean that societies have ceased to be differentiated and stratified. But nowhere does a ruling class derive its self-image from its opposition to the ruled; nowhere, except in insignificant pockets, is hegemony still a manifest matter of principle. Life has become too complex, the distribution of labor too universal, for the simple pattern of master and slave to lay any claim to validity. It is not the proofs of philosophers or the speeches of moralists that have brought about this world change; the power of the hitherto sovereign groups is too great, the violence of war too powerful, social distinctions too comprehensive, for sovereignty, war, and hegemony to continue to exist, although it may be assumed that it will be less a matter of simple elimination than of a change in the forms of these principles. There is no world power left today that could offer fundamental resistance to these changes.

This fundamental resistance was the very essence of fascist doctrines and powers. And this explains the sense in which one can speak of Hitler's epochal significance.

He seized upon the war, which in 1914 broke almost accidentally over a virtually pacifist world, with a passion and affirmation which were to have momentous consequences. It was no mere chance that he was the one to demarcate and thus to a certain extent create the *era of world wars*, for without him World War II would not have broken out, or at least not at that particular moment; without him the Soviet Union and the United States would in all likelihood have remained outside European history for decades to come. In this context, the era of world wars implies that period in which the means of warfare and communications were powerful enough to involve the whole earth in the struggle, but still weak enough to be accepted by a large number, particularly of leading men, and to be applied as a means of politics. Hitler can rightly be regarded as the central figure of this and *only* this era, while Lenin and Wilson transcend it in their significance.

At the same time it becomes apparent to what degree he has to share this prestige with others. He would have been a nationalist only, had the supranational social motive—the struggle against Marxism—not been a powerful and even decisive element in his actions. But this element had been developed by Mussolini in a manner far more significant because it was more authentic and less mythicizing. And Mussolini in turn certainly did not lack an analogous and perhaps even more interesting relationship to war. If fascism is regarded as a phenomenon belonging *only* to the era of the world wars, it is merely the accident of inferior means of power and a consequent lesser effectiveness that puts Mussolini in second place behind Hitler.

However, only of Hitler can it be said that he ended a far greater era because he brought its real fundamentals one by one to light and totally rejected its "ideological" nature. In this sense Hitler was a radical fascist and left Mussolini far behind.

Nevertheless, the earliest fascistoid thought trends emanated not from anxiety over war or the class structure of society, but from fear for the existing "culture." And obviously everything that had been called culture was produced by sovereign, martial, and self-antagonistic societies. It was a highly symptomatic event when one of the fathers of European socialism, Pierre Joseph Proudhon, acknowledged the cardinal and positive significance of war throughout history without insisting on its necessity for the future. Nietzsche's entire thinking is to be explained by this premise. His fundamental insight and anxiety was that "culture," as it had been created through the ages by privileged leisured classes, would no longer be able to exist in the basic change in the structure of society planned by liberals and socialists. He did not know yet that it can also have no abode in a fascist society, because its second and more vital root has been removed. Maurras' thinking is determined primarily by this anxiety for "culture," and this is why one can apply the term "early fascism" to his party.

This anxiety is present as an element in Hitler as well. He was no doubt sincere when he said that he was waging the war for the sake of a higher purpose—culture. But in comparison with Maurras one realizes how little weight and intrinsic value this element contains in Hitler's case, and the parallel with Mussolini has in turn shown that the development of the social motive was much less genuine with Hitler than with the Italian. It needs the combination of Maurras, Mussolini, and Hitler to show the complete, layered structure of the phenomenon; although the structure as a whole is present in each of them individually, it is not complete.

If this interpretation is correct, it should wipe out the impression that Hitler was a rather incomprehensible accident in the history of Germany and Europe. It becomes clear that he was possessed by "something," and that this "something" was in no sense casual or trivial. He no longer appears as an epochal figure but as the termination of an age. . . .

THE CONCEPT OF TRANSCENDENCE

Fascism has been defined on three levels. On the first level it was examined as an internal political phenomenon and described as "anti-Marxism" seeking to destroy the enemy by the development of a radically opposed yet related ideology and the application of nearly identical, although typically transformed methods; always, however, within the unyielding framework of national self-assertion and autonomy. This definition is valid for all forms of fascism.

The second definition, which describes fascism as the "life-and-death struggle of the sovereign, martial, inwardly antagonistic group," no longer looks at it as a manifestation within politics, but sees in it the natural foundation of politics itself brought to light and to self-consciousness. This definition could only be unequivocally demonstrated by the radical-fascist form and could be adequately illustrated within the context of this derivation.

On the third level—the least accessible and the most fundamental—fascism was termed "resistance to transcendence." This definition could be derived from fascism's oldest as well as its most recent forms: it describes fascism as a metapolitical phenomenon. It can be neither illustrated by historical details nor demonstrated by simple considerations. It requires a new departure in thought if it is not to remain a mere suggestion in the semiobscurity of approximate insight.

The historical section of this analysis was completed with the definition of fascism on internal and external political levels; the third level has hardly been touched, let alone demarcated. To grasp the phenomenon in its entirety, a final step must be taken and the nature of fascism explored in purely philosophical terms, even if only in outline and despite the danger that the object may seem to disappear for a time and that the striving for abstraction may mean sacrificing the support of demonstrable evidence. Nevertheless, this abstraction is no airy speculation. It is the means of probing to the hidden foundations of the structure. For in these foundations are situated all the complexity, all the tensions, of the edifice. It is not a featureless, uniform basis: on the contrary, it has its own characteristic measurements and proportions, and it is these which this method of abstraction seeks to uncover.

It becomes clear that this third approach is not simply an appendage which could just as well be left out when it is realized that the three definitions are something more than unconnected links in a random pile of associations. From certain aspects the first definition already contains the second, and a concept as central as that of ideology in turn requires the context of the second definition in order to achieve final clarification. The second definition for its part is irresistibly propelled toward the third, since politics itself is not a political fact and can only be manifested as such when set off against a foil whose nature differs from its own.

However, we are not setting foot on this third level for the first time. It was disclosed long ago as an element of the phenomenon itself. The most central of Maurras' ideas have been seen to penetrate to this level. By "monotheism" and "antinature" he did not imply a political process: he related these terms to the tradition of Western philosophy and religion, and left no doubt that for him they were adjuncts not only of Rousseau's notion of liberty but also of the Christian Gospels and Parmenides' concept of being. It is equally obvious that he regarded the unity of world economics, technology, science, and emancipation merely as another and more recent form of this "antinature." It was not difficult to find a place for Hitler's ideas as a cruder and more recent expression of this schema. Maurras' and Hitler's real enemy was seen to be "freedom toward the infinite" which, intrinsic in the individual and a reality in evolution, threatens to destroy the familiar and the beloved. From all this it begins to be apparent what is meant by "transcendence."

Wolfgang Sauer

FASCISM AS THE REVOLT OF "THE LOSERS"

Wolfgang W. Sauer (b. Berlin, 1920) graduated in History from the Free University of Berlin. He came to the United States in 1964 and is now Professor of Modern History at the University of California, Berkeley. The author of a number of writings on German and Central European history, he is particularly interested in the history and theory of civil-military relations.

. . . In Nazism, the historian faces a phenomenon that leaves him no way but rejection, whatever his individual position. . . . Does not such fundamental rejection imply a fundamental lack of understanding? And if we do not understand, how can we write history? The term "understanding" has, certainly, an ambivalent meaning; we can reject and still "understand." And yet, our intellectual, and psychological, capacities reach, in the case of Nazism, a border undreamed of by Wilhelm Dilthey. We can work out explanatory theories, but, if we face the facts directly, all explanations appear weak.

Thus, the attempt to write the history of Nazism confronts the historian with an apparently unsolvable dilemma and raises the question of what historical understanding and historical objectivity may mean in the face of Nazism. One of the merits of the totalitarianism theory was that it took care of this condition; from this point of view, one might be tempted to define it as a scholarly formulation of our lack of understanding.

Is there a better way to conceal our weakness? Among the established concepts one remains: fascism. To be sure, the theory of fascism has also suffered severely from both the politics of and the historical studies

From *Wolfgang Sauer, "National Socialism: Totalitarianism or Fascism?"* American Historical Review, LXXIII, no. 2 *(December 1967), 408–22. By permission of the author.*

on Nazism. This concerned, however, the Marxist-Leninist interpretation of fascism, and it may be worthwhile to ask if this interpretation is the only possible one. Attempts have indeed been made recently to repair the damaged tool for use. . . .

. . . A summary is naturally difficult in view of the differences in individual positions, and yet there are two closely related points of agreement. First, the authors agree that fascism is not, as the Marxist interpretation holds, merely a manipulation by monopoly capitalists: it is a mass movement with a character and aim of its own, indicating a major crisis in liberal democracy and capitalism. Whether or not this crisis is temporary remains controversial. Second, it is now established beyond doubt that the lower middle classes, both rural and urban, were at least one of the major social components of fascist movements. . . .

. . . This is, indeed, an important issue since the concept of the lower middle class still needs clarification, both in itself and in relation to the varieties of fascist supporters. Historical evidence shows that support of fascism may not be confined to the classical elements of the lower middle class (*Mittelstand*—peasants, artisans, small businessmen, and so forth), but may extend to a wide variety of groups in the large field between the workers on the one hand and big business, the aristocracy, and the top levels of bureaucracy on the other. This evidence agrees, interestingly enough, with Leo Baeck's statement that it was among the workers, the aristocracy, and the upper strata of the civil servants that the Jews found strongest support against persecution in Germany.[1]

Important as such an analysis is, however, it is still incomplete; it neglects the military element as a major social component of fascist movements. The military is apparently still not a category for social analysts. . . . It may even be said that a distinct interest group was formed within the fascist mixture by what might be called the military desperadoes, veterans of the First World War and the postwar struggles, who had not been reintegrated into either the civilian society or the armed forces. In an age of mass armies they were a sizable minority. Having become primitive warriors in four years and more of struggles, they sought to return into the arms of the mother army and to reform it according to their own model. Their conflict with society was, hence, not mainly economic, though this factor certainly was not absent. The main conflict was that between militarism and pacifism. In a time when the League of Nations appealed to the widespread war-weariness and

[1] *Das Dritte Reich und die Juden,* ed. Leon Poliakov and Josef Wulf (Berlin, 1955), p. 439.

the rising pacifism of the masses, the military desperadoes fought, not only for their own survival, but for the survival of soldiery in general.

The desperadoes were, thus, natural participants in the fascist revolution, but they did not merge entirely in the movement. Both in Italy and Germany the social differentiation was reflected in varying degrees in organizational differentiations between the party and the militia or the *sturmabteilung* (SA), respectively. This indicates that the conflict over militarism reemerged in varied form within the fascist movements. What was a conflict of principles in the relationship between the military desperadoes and society was a conflict of preferences in the fascist movements. The lower-middle-class groups and the military desperadoes considered each other as tools. The lower-middle-class members regarded the military desperadoes as a weapon to force their way into government; the military desperadoes hoped that the lower-middle-class members would provide the mass basis without which they could not expect to rule.

After the seizure of power the smoldering conflict within the fascist movements had to be resolved if the fascist regimes were to last. In Germany the conflict was terminated by Hitler when, in June 1934, he crushed the Röhm "revolt" which was . . . predominantly a movement of the military desperadoes. . . .

The control fascist regimes achieved over the dynamism of their movements creates doubts concerning the revolutionary character of fascist movements. There is virtual agreement among scholars that fascist movements contained, contrary to the Marxist thesis, a true revolutionary potential. This seems to conflict, however, with the noted opportunism of these movements. . . . A look at the fascist regimes in operation, moreover, would show that, whatever the revolutionary potential of the movements, the revolutionary results were meager.

How can this problem be resolved? May an answer be found by setting fascism in a wider historical framework? This is the way Nolte approaches his subject, but his answer is suggestive rather than conclusive. He advances the thesis that fascism was a revolt against the universal process of secularization, democratization, and international integration in the modern era. When this process reached its critical stage in the period of the two world wars, those elements in the culture that were doomed to perish revolted, according to Nolte, with increasing radicalism and decreasing rationality, or, in national terms, from the French *Action Française* through Italian Fascism to German National Socialism. On the last, most radical stage, fascism turned, Nolte argues, into a resistance against what he calls the "transcendence." He does not succeed, however, in clarifying this point sufficiently.

Nolte's thesis is not new in terms of facts. Its originality lies in assigning a metaphysical dimension to the fascist revolt and definitely attaching this revolt to a historical period. Fascism, Nolte suggests, is dead. This is, on the one hand, a more optimistic variation of the totalitarianism analysis; on the other hand, he tries to ascribe a historical meaning to fascism, which would provide a starting point for historical understanding. Much of this remains abstract and vague, however—mere *Ideengeschichte*. If the modernization process was universal, was fascist revolt also universal? If so, why does Nolte deal only with France, Italy, and Germany? If not, why did the fascist revolt occur only in these (and some other) countries? And what was the cause for differentiation? Why was this revolt most radical in Germany? Or, to put the question in a sociological rather than a national form, which social groups provided the mass basis of fascism, and why were just these groups antimodernist in their orientation? Why did the antimodernist fascist revolt frequently foster industrialization? And, finally, what exactly does "transcendence" mean, and by which concrete means did the fascist resistance against it manifest itself?

Nolte's neglect of these questions can be attributed primarily to his method, which he calls "phenomenological" and which he conceives as an attempt to return to G. W. F. Hegel's integration of philosophy and history. This attempt is, however, problematical. Hegel's striking success in synthesizing philosophy and history depended on his dialectical "logic"; Nolte's method is not dialectical. Nor does Nolte develop an alternative. He has not succeeded, therefore, in invalidating Leopold von Ranke's argument against Hegel that philosophy in itself does not produce a method for the analysis and organization of empirical facts. Philosophy alone was, indeed, not sufficient for Nolte; his phenomenological method turns out, under scrutiny, to be essentially Dilthey's good, old method of empathy, supplemented by some fragmentary social-scientific concepts formed ad hoc to satisfy immediate needs.

To be sure, Nolte makes this method operative by confining his study mainly to an interpretation of the ideas of the fascist leaders—Charles Maurras, Mussolini, Hitler—and he achieves much in this way, especially with regard to psychological and ideological analysis. Such a biographical approach is too narrow, however, to support Nolte's generalizations. What is true of the fascist leaders is not necessarily true of the masses of their followers. Their attitudes and motivation can be recognized only by a social analysis that includes economic factors.

Nolte would perhaps respond to such a suggestion with as much contempt as he shows for the use of the concept of industrialization. What does his concept of "practical transcendence" mean, however, if not that economic factors have adopted in modern societies a significance that transcends their "materialistic" meaning? And if this is true, how can we expect to gain meaningful results about modern societies without taking these factors into account? Nolte's method, in fact, seems to conflict heavily with his concept of "practical transcendence."

This must raise some doubts about the origin of Nolte's thesis of fascism as an antimodernist revolt. Indeed, he seems to have obtained his thesis, not through his biographical analyses, but rather through an analysis of Maurras's ideas. Nolte's decision, not too plausible at first glance, to raise the *Action Française* to a prominent position in the history of the origins of fascism, has, actually, methodological rather than historical reasons. The *Action Française* is important to Nolte because Maurras succeeded in building an intellectual bridge between the counterrevolutionary tradition and fascism, thereby establishing a unified concept of antimodernism that Nolte found apparently suggestive as an analytical concept for his own study. His chapter on the *Action Française* is, thus, actually a part of his methodological introduction.

The conclusion that Nolte arrived at his thesis in a methodologically irregular way does not necessarily imply that the thesis is wrong. It does imply, however, that he has not proven his case. Fascism and counterrevolution are actually different social phenomena, the latter being the earlier position of a part of what has been defined here as the allies of fascism. Fascism had its own independent antecedents: pseudo-revolutionaries like Father Jahn and the anti-Semites of the 1880s and 1890s (as examples in Germany). To be sure, counterrevolution showed a combination of revolutionary and reactionary elements similar to fascism, but it was a revolution from above while fascism is a revolution from below. The discussion of Maurras by Nolte explains, therefore, the possibility of the fascist-conservative alliance, but it does not explain fascism. Nor does Nolte provide a satisfying answer to the question of the origins of fascism, especially in the German case. Nolte's chapters on pre-1914 Germany and Austria are in fact among the weakest in his book, though this is owing partly to Nolte's general weakness in historical knowledge.

These criticisms do not, however, detract from the value of the book, which is a major step forward in the study of fascism. If verified, Nolte's hypothesis can offer, for example, an explanation for the fascist tendencies in the military; its metaphysical implications might, in addition, open a way to understand certain aspects in the relationship between the churches and fascism. Nolte might indeed have achieved his aim of developing a comprehensive theory of fascism had it not been for his mistaken conception of the relationship of philosophy and history and his refusal to consider the socioeconomic aspects of the problem.

The task is, then, to provide the non-Marxist theory of fascism with a socioeconomic dimension; more precisely, the task is to bring the earlier attempts of this kind up to date. Some contributors to the discussion in the 1930s have already laid important foundations for a socioeconomic theory of fascism. We have only to adjust these foundations to today's advanced stage of practical experience, historical research, and theoretical thought. With regard to theory the most important recent contribution probably comes from economic historians who have worked out, on the basis of the experiences of both the Great Depression and the underdeveloped countries, a non-Marxist concept of economic development that is highly suggestive to the analysis of fascism.

The attempt to use this concept for the interpretaion of fascism poses, of course, certain problems. The Marxist trap of economic determinism is but a minor difficulty. Apart from the fact that the difference between causes and conditions in social developments has meanwhile become sufficiently familiar to social scientists, it must also be stressed that the main purpose in using, here, an economic theory for a historical analysis is merely a heuristic one. In addition, the "theory of economic growth" is, in the last analysis, not strictly an economic theory. It is rather a historical synthesis of the process of industrialization on the basis of a socioeconomic analysis. Consequently, it already implies that the relationship between social and economic factors is a reversible one. In applying this theory to the interpretation of fascism, we merely shift the perspective without abandoning reversibility.

A more important problem arises because we have to face, as usual, several conflicting formulations of that theory. Only those formulations that focus on continental European conditions, however, are useful to the analysis of fascism. This reduces the number of alternatives to two: the models of Alexander Gerschenkron and W. W. Rostow. If we analyze the results of these two theories with regard to the social context of industrialization, we find that they are complementary. Gerschenkron's theory of "relative backwardness" provides a model of historical differentiation missing in Rostow's "stage" theory, and the latter offers a model for periodization not developed by Gerschenkron.

The critical problem is the development of a model for the advanced period of the industrialization process. Gerschenkron's model of relative backwardness cannot be directly extended to it since it deals with the starting conditions, while Rostow's definition as a stage of "high mass consumption" is still unsatisfactory.[2] Rostow hits, certainly, the essential point: that industry, if it exceeds a certain limit of growth, must turn to mass production. He is also aware that private mass consumption is not the only possible response. Rostow's idea, however, that societies on the stage of mass production have a choice between high mass consumption and national political expansion (or, between private mass consumption and mass consumption by the state), does not entirely agree with the historical evidence. There is certainly an element of choice in the situation; yet it may well be that there are also constraints working against a choice. They may be owing to the consequences of relative backwardness, or to differential national developments and resulting international tensions and crises such as war. Rostow neglects the impact of national economic growth on international relations and vice versa; this seems to be, in fact, the major weakness of his theory. If we analyze twentieth-century history from this point of view, we do indeed find a period of world crises (World War I, the Great Depression, World War II) spreading between Rostow's stages of industrial maturity and high mass consumption.

In terms of a theory of economic growth revised in this way, fascism can be defined as a revolt of those who lost—directly or indirectly, temporarily or permanently—by industrialization. Fascism is a revolt of the *déclassés*. The workers and industrialists do not fall under this definition; it applies mainly to most of the lower middle class as defined above. They indeed suffered, or feared they would suffer, from industrialization —peasants who opposed the urbanizing aspects of industrialism; small businessmen and those engaged in the traditional crafts and trades that opposed mechanization or concentration; white-collar workers (at least as long as they felt the loss of economic independence); lower levels of the professions, especially the teaching profession, which opposed changing social values; and so forth. Also the military joins here, with opposition against the industrialization of war, which tended to destroy traditional modes of warfare and which by its increasing destructiveness intensified pacifism and antimilitarism. On the other hand, groups like the aristocracy, the large landlords, the higher bureaucrats, and so on, who lost also by industrialization, generally did not turn to fascism. In continuing the counterrevolutionary position, they defended hierarchical society and abhorred, therefore, the egalitarian elements in fascism. In

---

[2] Alexander Gerschenkron, *Economic Backwardness in Historical Perspective* (Cambridge, Mass., 1962), esp. pp. 1–51, 353–64; W. W. Rostow, *The Stages of Economic Growth* (Cambridge, Eng., 1959); *The Economics of Take-off into Sustained Growth*, ed. *id.* (London, 1963). Cf. the review by Henry Rosovsky, "The Take-off into Sustained Controversy," *Journal of Economic History*, XXV (1965), 271–75.

exact distinction, then, fascist movements represented the reaction of the lower-class losers, while the upper-class losers tended to react in a nonfascist way, but were potential allies of fascist regimes.

Such an analysis seems to be a way of explaining the intriguing paradox of a revolutionary mass movement whose goals were antirevolutionary in the classical sense. As a movement of losers, it turned against technological progress and economic growth; it tried to stop or even to reverse the trend toward industrialization and to return to the earlier, "natural" ways of life. In this respect the movement was reactionary, but, as a movement of the lower classes, its means were necessarily revolutionary. In defining fascism as a revolt of losers, we can also understand better both fascist atavism and fascist opportunism. Since the process of industrialization as a whole is irresistible, the existence of civilization is inextricably bound to it. Fascist revolt against industrialization must, therefore, eventually turn against civilization too. This was most evident in Germany, where Nazism developed into full-fledged neobarbarism, but it is also true of the other fascist movements, though for various reasons neobarbarism remained, there, more or less underdeveloped. Such a definition of fascism as a neobarbaric revolt against civilization seems to describe in more concrete terms what Nolte calls the resistance against the "transcendence."

The same condition led to fascist opportunism. Since fascists acted, as losers, essentially from a position of weakness, they were compelled, in spite of their tendency toward violence, to compromise with their environment, even with their industrial enemy. This accounts for the contradiction that fascist regimes often fostered industrialization and yet insisted, ultimately, upon setting the clock back. The dialectic that resulted from this condition led eventually to a point at which the movement assumed suicidal proportions. Industrialization was sought in order to destroy industrial society, but since there was no alternative to industrial society, the fascist regime must eventually destroy itself. This was the situation of Nazism. The Nazis built an industrial machinery to murder the Jews, but once in operation the machine would have had to continue and would have ruined, indirectly at least, first the remnants of civilized society and then the fascist regime. Industrialization of mass murder was, thus, the only logical answer Nazism had to the problems of industrial society.

The analysis of fascism in terms of economic growth also offers a way to define more precisely the fallacy in the Marxist-Leninist concept of fascism. The fallacy lies in that Marxism blurs the distinction between early commercial and late industrial capitalism. Fascism indicated a conflict within capitalism, between traditional forms of commercialism and the modern form of industrialism. The fact that the former had survived in the twentieth century only on the lower levels of the middle classes accounted for the social locus of fascism. It is true, therefore, that fascism was capitalist by nature; it is not true that it was industrial. It is also true that fascist regimes often were manipulated in varying ways and degrees, but the share of industrialists in manipulation was rather small. Fetscher shows convincingly that the share was indeed larger in industrially underdeveloped Italy than it was in industrially advanced Germany.

On the other hand, the difference between fascism and Bolshevism appears, in light of this analysis, more fundamental than the totalitarianism analysis would admit. Neither V. I. Lenin nor Joseph Stalin wished to turn the clock back; they not merely wished to move ahead, but they wished to jump ahead. The Bolshevik revolution had many elements of a development revolution not unlike those now under way in the under-developed countries. One of the striking differences between the two systems appears in the role of the leaders. The social and political order of Bolshevism is relatively independent from the leadership; it is, so to speak, more objective. Fascist regimes, by contrast, are almost identical with their leaders; no fascist regime has so far survived its leader. This is why Bullock's interpretation of Hitler in terms of traditional tyranny has some bearing. The limits of this approach would become evident, I believe, if scholars could be persuaded to balance their interest in Hitler's secret utterances and political and military scheming by also stressing his role as a public speaker. The Nazi mass rallies with their immediate, ecstatic communication between leader and followers were, indeed, what might be called a momentary materialization of the Nazi utopia, at least so far as the "Nordic race" was concerned.

Finally, it is plain from an analysis in terms of economic growth that the degree of radicalization must somehow be related to the degree of industrialization. The more highly industrialized a society, the more violent the reaction of the losers. Thus Germany stood at the top, Italy lagged behind, and Spain and others were at the bottom. In Germany, fascism gained sufficient momentum to oust its allies. By the dismissal of Schacht, Werner von Blomberg, Werner von Fritsch, and Konstantin von Neurath in 1937–38, the Nazis assumed control over the economy, the army, and the diplomacy, those exact three positions that their con-servative allies of January 30, 1933, had deemed it most important to maintain. In Italy a fairly stable balance was sustained between the movement and its various allies until the latter, relying on the monarchy and assisted by Fascism's defeat in war, finally ousted the Fascists. In Spain, a borderline case, the allies assumed control from the outset and never abandoned it. Similar observations can be made with the many cases of pre-, proto-, and pseudofascist regimes in Central, Eastern, and Southeastern Europe.

The thesis of the parallel growth of industrialization and fascist radicalization seems to conflict, however, with the evidence of some highly industrialized societies such as France and England where fascist opposition never gained much momentum. The problem can be solved only by adding a broader historical analysis involving the specific national, social, and cultural traditions that industrialization encountered in individual societies. It is perhaps not accidental that the industrialization process ran relatively smoothly in West European nations whose political rise concurred with the rise of modern civilization since the late Middle Ages. Fascist opposition, by contrast, was strongest in the Mediterranean and Central European regions where the premodern traditions of the ancient Roman and the medieval German and Turkish Empires persisted. The religious division between Protestantism and Catholicism may also have some relevance: one remembers both Max Weber's thesis on the correlation of Protestantism and capitalism and the recent controversy on the attitude of Pope Pius XII toward Fascism and Nazism. In other words, fascism emerged where preindustrial traditions were both strongest and most alien to industrialism and, hence, where the rise of the latter caused a major break with the past and substantial losses to the nonindustrial classes.

This definition is still incomplete, however, since it does not tell why fascism emerged rather simultaneously throughout Europe though the countries affected were on different levels of economic growth. We face here the question of the "epoch" of fascism, raised but not answered by Nolte. The general conditions of fascism as defined above existed, after all, earlier. In Germany, for example, lower-middle-class opposition against industrialization had already emerged in the mid-nineteenth century and accompanied economic growth in varying degrees through all its stages. Why did it not turn into fascism prior to 1914, though it did so on parallel stages of growth in Italy and Spain after the First World War? At this point the importance of the military element for the analysis of fascism becomes apparent again: Only after total war had militarized European societies and had created large military interests were the conditions required for fascism complete. The First World War had tremendously strengthened industrialization in technical terms, but it had diverted it from production to destruction. After the war the victorious nations of the West managed, on the whole, to stabilize industrial society and to return to production, but the defeated nations and those industrially underdeveloped found it extremely difficult to follow the same course. When they met with economic crises, many of them abandoned whatever advance they had made toward democracy and turned to fascism.

This breakdown occurred roughly along the social and cultural lines defined above. If we examine the geographical distribution of fascist regimes in Europe between the two world wars, we find that they emerged mainly in three areas: the Mediterranean coast; the regions of Central, Eastern, and Southeastern Europe; and Germany. In the first area, the original and highly developed Mediterranean urban and commercial civilization that reached back to antiquity faced destruction by the invasion of industrialism as released or accelerated by World War I. Defeat, either imagined as in the case of Italy or real as in the case of Spain at the hands of Abd-el-Krim at Anual in 1921, played an additional role. In the second area, an old feudal civilization struggled with the problems arising out of sudden liberation from Habsburg or tsarist dominations as well as from competition with both Western industrialism and Eastern Bolshevism. Both regions were predominantly Catholic. In the third area, a technologically fully developed industrial society clashed violently with the stubborn resistance of surviving remnants of preindustrial forms of society over who was to pay for defeat and economic crises. Catholicism played, here, a dual and partly contradictory role. On the one hand, it seems to have influenced indirectly Nazism as such top Nazi leaders as Hitler, Himmler, and Goebbels were Catholic by origin, and the Vatican was quick to compromise with the Hitler regime. On the other hand, the vast majority of the Catholic population was relatively immune to Nazi temptations. Significantly enough, Protestantism also split, though along somewhat different lines.

These differentiations suggest a division into three subtypes of fascism: the Mediterranean as the "original" one; the various and not too long-lived regimes in Central, Eastern, and Southeastern Europe as a mixed, or not full-fledged, variation; and German Nazism as a special form.

The "epoch" of fascism starts, thus, with the aftermath of the First World War, but when does it end? Eugen Weber and Lipset agree with many scholars who believe that there is no epoch of fascism, that fascism is a general condition of modern society contingent upon crises in liberal democracy. This is certainly indisputable as far as fascist attitudes and movements are concerned; it is quite another problem, however, whether fascist regimes will emerge again. This emergence seems unlikely for two reasons. First, the socioeconomic development in the highly industrialized societies of the West generally rules out the reemergence of the historical condition of fascism—a disarrangement of society in which the rise of large masses of *déclassés* coincides with the rise of a sizable group of military desperadoes. There are no longer economic losers of industrialization, at least not on a mass scale, and Charles de Gaulle's victory over the rebellious French military shows that military desperadoes alone will not get very far.[3] In addition, the horrible experience of neobarbarism puts a heavy burden on all attempts at imitation. If the success of fascism under modern, Western conditions is unlikely, there remain, theoretically, the underdeveloped countries as possible breeding grounds of fascism. Yet it is doubtful whether opposition against industrialization will assume there the form of fascism since these countries lack the specific traditions of the ancient and medieval civilizations that conditioned the antimodernist revolt in Europe. The second reason working against fascist regimes is, thus, that fascism is inseparable from its Central and South European conditions; it is, in fact, one of the products of the dialectical movement of European civilization.

[3] It would be different in case of large-scale war which might, of course, drastically change present social conditions.

SUGGESTED READINGS ON INTERNATIONAL FASCISM

There is now an abundant literature in English on fascism in Italy and Germany, but a still insufficient number of sources on the movements in the other Western nations, and very little on the fascists in the countries of Eastern Europe. Studies on fascism as an international phenomenon have been particularly limited in number, with the works reprinted in this volume representing the best speculative thought on the subject. Students wishing to read further can begin with F. L. Carsten's *The Rise of Fascism* (Berkeley, 1969), a general survey based mainly on secondary sources and concluding with a selected bibliography on the various national parties. An important collection of specialized articles appears in *International Fascism: 1920–1945* (New York, 1966), a paperback issue of the *Journal of Contemporary History*, I, no. 1 (1966), edited by George L. Mosse and Walter Laqueur. A helpful series of more general articles surveying many of the national movements is found in *European Fascism* (London, 1968), edited by S. J. Woolf. The latter can be supplemented by the topical essays in Professor Woolf's *The Nature of Fascism* (London, 1968), being the papers and discussions of a conference on fascism held at Reading University, England, in 1967. The contributions to *The European Right: A Historical Profile* (Berkeley, 1965), edited by Eugen Weber and Hans Rogger, are also relevant. A. J. Gregor attempts to find clarity in fascist thought in his somewhat murky *The Ideology of Fascism* (New York, 1969). Two works, the second more satisfying than the first, trace developments to the present: Dennis Eisenberg, *The Re-emergence of Fascism* (London, 1967), and Angelo Del Boca and Mario Giovana,

Fascism Today (New York, 1969); and two collections have appeared with readings from primary and secondary sources: Nathanael Greene, ed., *Fascism: An Anthology* (New York, 1968), and John Weiss, ed., *Nazis and Fascists in Europe: 1918–1945* (New York, 1969).

The themes developed in the first section of this volume can be studied further in the writings of the 1930s and early war years. The official Stalinist interpretation of fascism is fully developed in the report and speeches of the former General Secretary of the Comintern to the Seventh World Congress: Georgi Dimitrov, *The Working Class Against Fascism* (London, 1935). Different shades of Marxist and socialist opinion in the Western countries appear in Daniel Guérin (French), *Fascism and Big Business* (New York, 1939); Harold J. Laski (English), *Where Do We Go From Here?* (New York, 1940); and Norman Thomas (American), *Fascism or Socialism?* (New York, 1934). The most remarkable Marxist analysis, Franz Neumann, *Behemoth: The Structure and Practice of National Socialism* (New York, 1944), concerns only the German model, as does the most stimulating conservative interpretation: Hermann Rauschning, *The Revolution of Nihilism* (New York, 1939). A view from above politics—or so it is claimed— is Karl Mannheim's *Man and Society in an Age of Reconstruction* (London, 1940), a work revealing the sociological imagination at its best.

The totalitarian school of interpretation has produced a rich and varied literature. Critical bibliographies can be found in Carl J. Friedrich and Zbigniew K. Brzezinski, *Totalitarian Dictatorship and Autocracy* (Cambridge, Mass., 1956), and Paul T. Mason, *Totalitarianism: Temporary Madness or Permanent Danger?* (Boston, 1967). The original outlines of the idea are contained in Sigmund Neumann, *Permanent Revolution* (New York, 1942), and are given comprehensive form in Carl J. Friedrich, ed., *Totalitarianism: Proceedings of a Conference Held at the American Academy of Arts and Sciences, March, 1953* (Cambridge, Mass., 1954). Further reading, however, should begin with Hannah Arendt's brilliant *The Origins of Totalitarianism* (New York, 1951), which sets the concept in the historical perspective of the late nineteenth century. J. L. Talmon traces the ideological roots back further in the somewhat forced arguments of his *The Origins of Totalitarian Democracy* (New York, 1952). Speculation on the psychological aspects of the problem are found in T. W. Adorno, et al., *The Authoritarian Personality* (New York, 1950), and Zevedei Barbu, *Democracy and Dictatorship* (New York, 1956). More recent reflections on the notion of totalitarianism are found in Hans Buchheim, *Totalitarian Rule: Its Nature and Characteristics* (Middletown, Conn., 1968), and Carl

J. Friedrich, Michael Curtis, and Benjamin R. Barber, *Totalitarianism in Perspective: Three Views* (New York, 1969).

Attempts to understand fascism as a twentieth-century expression of certain universal historical traditions have resulted in a number of interesting studies. Alfred Cobban's *Dictatorship: Its History and Theory* (London, 1939), places the fascist regimes in the line of classical and modern dictatorships. More recent and less historical is Maurice Latey, *Tyranny* (London, 1969). Here again, however, the most durable work is on the National Socialist experience: Alan Bullock, *Hitler: A Study in Tyranny* (New York, 1953). Connections between fascism and the darker influences of Platonic thought are explored by Karl R. Popper, *The Open Society and Its Enemies* (London, 1945); and Norman Cohn discovers links with millennialism in his brilliant study of the messianic sects of medieval and reformation Europe: *The Pursuit of the Millennium* (New York, 1957). Fascism is seen as a form of "integral nationalism," a synthesis of earlier nationalist traditions, in Carlton J. H. Hayes, *The Historical Evolution of Modern Nationalism* (New York, 1931). George L. Mosse, a noted authority on the ideological origins of National Socialism, connects fascism with the triumph of irrational and authoritarian influences from the nineteenth century over their rational and liberal alternatives: *The Culture of Western Europe* (Chicago, 1961). The theme of fascism as the breakthrough of Germanic Romanticism over Mediterranean classicism is argued in the case of Nazism by Peter Viereck, *Metapolitics. From the Romantics to Hitler* (New York, 1941). Finally the identification of fascism as a radical form of traditional political protest can be further studied in two of the works cited above: Weber and Rogger, *The European Right*, and S. J. Woolf, *European Fascism*. On the same theme, René Rémond's *The Right Wing in France from 1815 to de Gaulle* (Philadelphia, 1966) offers observations which are relevant beyond French politics.

The significance of fascism in the modernization process is considered by several contributors to Woolf's *The Nature of Fascism*, and especially by A. F. K. Organski, "Fascism and Modernization." The same author offers further reflections in his *The Stages of Political Growth* (New York, 1965). Although limited to the subject of Nazism, two books should be mentioned for their minority view that fascism was a force for modernization, despite its own paradoxical intention to destroy the modern industrial state: David Schoenbaum, *Hitler's Social Revolution* (New York, 1966), and Ralf Dahrendorf, *Society and Democracy in Germany* (Garden City, N.Y., 1967). For some neo-Marxist thoughts to the contrary, see the writings of T. W. Mason, including his article in Woolf's collection last cited, "The Primacy of Politics and Economics in National Socialist Germany." Students interested in the full scope of the problem, however, should begin with the remaining chapters of Barrington Moore's *Social Origins of Dictatorship and Democracy*, the most imaginative work on the connection between politics and modernization.

SOURCES OF CIVILIZATION IN THE WEST

Robert Lee Wolff, *General Editor*

The Age of Imperialism, *edited by Robin W. Winks*, S-205

The Ancient World: Justice, Heroism, and Responsibility, *edited by Zeph Stewart*, S-141

Century of Genius: European Thought 1600–1700, *edited by Richard T. Vann*, S-149

The Conversion of Western Europe, 350–750, *edited by J. N. Hillgarth*, S-203

The Crisis of Church & State, 1050–1300, *by Brian Tierney* (*with selected documents*), S-102

The English Reform Tradition 1790–1910, *edited by Sydney W. Jackman*, S-120

The Enlightenment, *edited by Frank E. Manuel*, S-121

The French Revolution, *edited by Philip Dawson*, S-161

The High Middle Ages, 814–1300, *edited by Archibald R. Lewis*, S-204

Icon and Minaret: Sources of Byzantine and Islamic Civilization, *edited by Charles M. Brand*, S-199

The Image of Rome, *edited by Erich S. Gruen*, S-194

The Italian Renaissance, *edited by Werner L. Gundersheimer*, S-128

Nineteenth Century Thought: The Discovery of Change, *edited by Richard L. Schoenwald*, S-129

The Protestant Reformation, *edited by Lewis W. Spitz*, S-140